Needs, Rights, and the Market

Needs, Rights, and the Market

David Levine

Lynne Rienner Publishers • Boulder and London

Published in the United States of America in 1988 by
Lynne Rienner Publishers, Inc.
948 North Street, Boulder, Colorado 80302

and in the United Kingdom by
Lynne Rienner Publishers, Inc.
3 Henrietta Street, Covent Garden, London WC2E 8LU

Library of Congress Cataloging-in-Publication Data
Levine, David P., 1948–
    Needs, rights, and the market / by David P. Levine.
        p.   cm.
    Bibliography: p.
    Includes index.
    ISBN 1-55587-115-1 (lib. bdg.)
    1. Capitalism.   2. Consumers.   3. Property.
    4. Income distribution.   I. Title.
HB501.L397 1988
330—dc19   88-4543
                                                                CIP
British Library Cataloguing in Publication Data
A Cataloguing in Publication record for this book
is available from the British Library.

Printed and bound in the United States of America

The paper used in this publication meets
the requirements of the American National
Standard for Permanence of Paper for
Printed Library Materials Z39.48-1984. ∞

CONTENTS

PREFACE

This is a book about the market, about what the market does for us, and about the limits we ought to place on it. The book addresses long-standing and much debated questions of political economy: How do markets work and what is their social purpose? What sorts of wants are appropriate for us to satisfy through the use of markets? What limits can we legitimately place on property right and the exchange of property? What is the relation between inequality of income and wealth and inequality of persons? How do we reconcile the demands of liberty with those of welfare?

In part, these are questions about the economy and because of this we should expect an important contribution from economics in our search for answers. I was educated to become an economist and little in this book fails to remind me of the strengths and weaknesses of that education. In many ways the contribution of economics (especially the great tradition of the classical economists) to this book has been substantial. Yet, as valuable as that contribution has been, it is also, I think, deeply flawed.

When economists deal with the way the market works, they begin by making assumptions about what motivates people to work together in producing and distributing the things they need. Economics does not as a rule delve deeply into human motivation. Economists concern themselves much more with the implications of assumptions about motives than with the motives themselves. Bearing in mind the limited objectives of economics, I have no argument to make against this approach. We cannot accomplish everything at once. If separating out a part of the problem somewhat in isolation assures that we will make some mistakes it also assures us the chance that we might make some progress. If our notion of human motivation is sound then an economics resting, however uncritically, upon that notion might serve us well. But if our notion of human motivation is not sound, our understanding of how the economy works based on that notion will serve us poorly. I wrote this book out of a conviction that the ideas economists work with regarding why people do what they do and want what they want are fundamentally unsound. They and the economics based on them have not served us well.

I will not attempt to support this assertion here, or subsequently in this book. I talk about it in the first chapter, but I present no comprehensive arguments. I mainly assert the weakness of the traditional idea and go ahead to interpret economic life on a different basis. This seems to me a sensible procedure, although I know it will annoy many of those wedded to more traditional ways of thinking about the economy. Those more traditionally minded might expect me to deal at length with their ideas and with the relationship those ideas bear to my own. Doing so is not part of my purpose in this book. Better, I think, to get on with the work of testing the power of our ideas against their ability to illuminate the important issues. This is what I do here. I assume, as economists do, a basic underlying framework for thinking about persons and then see how it helps to bring together a range of vital concerns in a meaningful way. I am satisfied that it does.

The fundamental idea that I work with is that individuals have (or attempt to develop) an enduring and coherent sense of themselves and that they try to make this sense of self real to others through a way or mode of life, including a mode of consumption. Sense of self and mode of life exist in a social context and consist of socially meaningful acts and ideas. I explore what this means for the treatment of what economists term "consumer behavior." I then pursue the implications of these ideas about the consumer for our understanding of consumer decisionmaking as that bears on the way markets work. This exploration provides a basis for a discussion of the nature of self-determination, the limits of property right, and the relation of need to right.

Simply put, we can characterize this idea in the following way: For the traditional approach our mode of consumption makes us more or less happy, but it does not really matter to us; it does not have to do with who we are in the world. In the framework of this book, consumption decisions matter. Those decisions implicate our way of life, and our way of life matters. The framework's ability to make individual decisions meaningful gives it strength. This strength lends conviction to the answers suggested for the questions in political economy posed above.

I am well aware that much of what I say in the following pages about the individual and the market might be said somehow in a more traditional framework—for example, one employing terms such as preference and choice. This strikes me as wholly beside the point. If what I say here can be said using the traditional language, it cannot be well said. The usual language prevents us from placing what I consider most important about the individual at the forefront of our understanding of him. The traditional image of the consumer, while in some ways familiar, strikes me as curiously empty; the closer we look at this image, the less we recognize ourselves in it. I hope that the interpretation put forward in the following pages is one through which we can see ourselves and our economic lives more clearly, one through which, in the words of R. G. Collingwood, we might "come to know better what to some extent we knew already" (*An Essay on Philosophical Method*, p. 205).

I would like to thank Avi Cohen, Carol Heim, Roscoe Hill, Lynn Levine, Tracy Mott, and Jeff Oxley for their criticisms of earlier drafts of this book. Lucy Ware provided substantial assistance in the preparation of the notes. Without encouragement from Jim Caporaso and Alan Gilbert, the book might not have been published. I greatly appreciate their support. Lynne Rienner and her staff made the manuscript into a book, and I especially appreciate that.

Between 1981 and 1986, while working on this project, I also headed a small academic experiment at the University of Denver. I would like to dedicate this book to the friends and colleagues who participated in or otherwise supported that experiment.

—*David Levine*

NEEDS 1

If it is said that the essential function of language is its capacity for poetry, we shall assume that the essential function of consumption is its capacity to make sense. Forget that commodities are good for eating, clothing and shelter; forget their usefulness and try instead the idea that commodities are good for thinking; treat them as a nonverbal medium for the human creative faculty.

—Mary Douglas and Baron Isherwood, *The World of Goods*

THE ECONOMY

When we think about an economy, we think of a set of relations by which we acquire the means to satisfy needs, but only certain kinds of needs. This qualification is very important. Some of our needs drive us into economic activities, others do not. When we ask what types of needs are appropriate for us to satisfy through economic activity, we question the boundaries that separate our economic life from other dimensions of our social condition (especially personal and political life). Problems of political economy involve these boundaries in important ways. When we consider the relation of needs to rights, we also take up the problem of determining the kinds of needs we satisfy at our will (by right), and the kinds of rights (e.g., property rights) that bear upon the economy. We will begin our analysis of needs and rights, then, with a closer study of the kinds of needs whose satisfaction involves economic activity.

If my intent is to satisfy a need I have for housing, then I enter

1

into a distinctively economic relation in order to acquire the necessary means: I purchase a house from an individual who owns one. In the course of the transaction, the individual who sells me the house expresses no particular interest in my reasons for purchasing it. On one level these reasons are obvious, on another they are no one's affair but my own.

If my intent is to change a law by which my life in society is governed (e.g., to make possession of firearms illegal except under certain restrictive circumstances), any private need (peculiarly my own) that would be satisfied with the law, but not without it, is essentially irrelevant. To be sure, my motives in advocating the specific law may stem from my perception of personal gain or loss. Nonetheless, the pursuit of a change in law will require me to argue for the worthiness of the new law on grounds independent of personal gain.

In politics, our purposes must be supported by reason; and other members of the body politic have every right (in a sense, they have an obligation) to demand and to scrutinize those reasons.[1] The contrast between political and economic affairs could not be sharper, and this sharpness remains even where private ends infect (i.e., corrupt) public affairs. In politics, we must convince others that our purposes are not, in substance, private. In economic relations we pursue the means to satisfy private needs; in political life, we attempt to define and achieve a public purpose.

In the following, we restrict our attention to those activities associated with the satisfaction of private needs, and seek to understand their distinctiveness. This restriction presupposes the validity of the distinction between self-interest and public purpose. While this distinction may have intuitive appeal, contemporary social science finds it deeply problematic.[2] In the following, part of our purpose will be to indicate a way in which private ends can be defined so as to leave room for the idea of a public purpose irreducible to the net outcome of the clash of self-interests. We do not, however, seek to take the next step and indicate the terms in which public purpose can be defined. While our analysis of the system of self-seeking should illuminate this closely related issue, it will not directly resolve it. It must be admitted that without a clear resolution of the issue, the assumption that we can clearly distinguish public purpose from private end remains questionable.

Given our distinction between private need and public purpose, a further distinction suggests itself. Economics studies the relations into which we enter in order to provide ourselves with the means to satisfy needs. These relations do not subsume the relations (and associated activities) by which we satisfy those needs.

When I acquire my house, the relations into which I enter are clearly economic. But when I go about living my life in my house, the relations into which I enter no longer have the same economic character. Other, essentially different, concerns and objectives take hold. Many of these concerns involve acts of consumption that bear an important relation to economic activities that provide the household with its means of consumption. How do the economic relations by which I acquire the means of consumption relate to the household relations (predominantly familial relations) of consuming those commodities my participation in the economy allows me to acquire?

In order to distinguish political from economic affairs, we employed the idea of an opposition between public and private. More specifically, we emphasized the difference between public purpose and personal need. If our idea of economic affairs as activities directed toward private ends makes sense, we have no choice but to think of the consumption of the means acquired through those activities as private, even personal. Such consumption realizes or achieves the end that directs us when we participate in economic affairs.

We now have a threefold division between the public, the private, and the public relations by which we pursue private ends. In order to clarify the distinction, consider the way an individual participates in these three kinds of relations.

Clearly, given the way we have defined it, public life allows little room for the exercise of individuality. Thus the act of joining a political party should in principle reflect a commitment to certain basic ideas having to do with the way society is to be governed. By joining a party (indeed, even by merely casting a vote), I assert the universal validity of these basic ideas. When I enter the political arena to advance certain ideas, I am in effect asserting that those ideas should be the governing principles of the whole of society, equally applicable to all of its members. Such ideas have no necessary connection to my individual or personal qualities. In arriving at these ideas, and in deducing their universal application, I abstract from those features of my personality that make me different from other members of the same body politic.

The opposite result follows when I enter into relations of consumption within my household. Here I am concerned with my particular person; I have a pressing need to attach means of consumption to my person and make them my property (what is proper to me as a particular individual). I am concerned that I differentiate myself from others. What I need, and what I do, cease to have the universal applicability associated with my political life.

I go out into the world to acquire the objects I need to sustain my life as a particular individual, objects destined to become my personal property. But before I acquire them, they have no special association with my personality, my needs, and my private life. Thus, prior to acquiring them, those objects must be defined without regard to my personality. Yet those same objects must have the capacity to develop a special relation to my person and to help support my individuality.

The activities that define the economy must go on without reference to any particular individual. Means of consumption must be produced and made available. But, while they must fulfill individual needs, they are produced and made available without any direct link to a particular person. The objects are simultaneously independent of and capable of supporting the most private qualities of a particular personality.

This peculiar mix of impersonal and personal defines the economy. In the following we consider the nature of a private need more closely in order to clarify the way the distinctiveness of individual personality is sustained within society.

NEED AND CHOICE

The idea of need implies the force of necessity. Put simply, a need is a requirement of life. This links the idea of need to that of purpose, and of the subordination of an object to the sustenance of an organism or a structure. Fish need the sea, cars need batteries, etc. When we say that a car needs a battery, we mean that it cannot behave like a car without one.

Does a person have needs? Or do cars and fish have needs only to the extent that they are biologically or mechanically determined? If we (mistakenly) view a person as a biological organism, we can isolate a set of genuine needs for determinate or at least minimum nutritional inputs and environmental compatibility (e.g., warmth). Yet it is very difficult to account for the major part of individual consumption by referring to such needs. The form in which we consume most objects and our motivation in consuming them can hardly be accounted for on the basis of the nutritional or other requirements of biological life. Thus our need for protein does not determine whether we consume fish or meat, fried chicken or bean curd.

The distinctiveness of the objects of individual consumption and of the purposes accomplished through individual consumption have led economists to give up the idea of need and to introduce a different concept with radically different implications. Rather than arguing that the individual has needs for means of consumption, the economist thinks of consumption as satisfying desires. Desires are distinguished from needs by the absence of the force of necessity. This absence expresses itself most clearly when economists argue, for purposes of economic analysis, that the decisive aspect of consumption is choice among ends.

An economist considering the relationship between the individual and his means of consumption does not consider the possibility that the individual needs those means. Instead, the economist thinks of the relation between individual and object as one in which the individual chooses the object because he prefers it to others. My need for an object implies that the integrity of my being depends on its acquisition. If I only prefer that object, then I must be capable of sustaining myself whether or not I acquire it. The acquisition and the consumption of the object may exercise individuality in a certain way, but the fundamental structure of the person is supported outside of the person's relation to means of consumption.

Thus, I may prefer a house to an apartment, but who I am does not in any way depend on which kind of shelter I actually inhabit. Only my overall level of satisfaction depends on the outcome of my economic pursuits; the more successful I am, the higher my degree of satisfaction. The kind of person I am remains the same regardless of what I consume.

To what extent are we forced to decide between need and preference in thinking about consumer behavior? Some economists have sought to include both types of motivation, applying each to its appropriate range of objects. This approach requires that we distinguish between two classes of objects: those the individual needs, and those the individual only prefers to have.

The roots of this idea take us back to the origins of economics. Indeed, the distinction between a part of the social product destined to satisfy needs and another destined to meet desires provided a basis for the first serious attempts to develop scientific accounts of economic behavior.[3] The part of the product that went to satisfy needs was termed subsistence, and what remained of the total product was variously termed luxury, riches, or wealth. Ultimately, the distinction was refined into one of subsistence and the net product. The distinction developed in different directions, but economists during this early period tended to emphasize the role played by subsistence in economic affairs. Consistent with this emphasis on subsistence, economists relegated luxury consumption to the status of a residual that played no active part in regulating economic activities.

So long as economics retained the notion of subsistence, the element of necessity continued to play an important part in consumption, and, in turn, had an effect across the range of economic affairs. Particularly in early theories of income distribution, the concept of the subsistence wage played a decisive role. Given the productivity of labor, the part of the product returned to the worker as his subsistence determined how much was available for investment and luxury consumption. Thus the idea of subsistence need lies at the core of the thinking of the founders of economic science.

Yet throughout the development of theories based on the idea of subsistence, a crucial question was neither expressly stated nor satisfactorily resolved: What determines the magnitude and the composition of subsistence? All the power of the idea of subsistence depends on the way in which it asserts that the consumer's needs are determinate. This result helps to determine what remains as net product. While economists who relied heavily on a notion of subsistence wages could use that idea to determine the net product, none was able to make any compelling statements regarding what determined the subsistence itself.

Inevitably, economists sought to link the magnitude of subsistence to some idea of the production (or reproduction) of the worker. This made the worker little more than a produced input. The worker may have directly produced the net product, but its ultimate source was the subsistence goods whose consumption "produced" the worker. Once the worker becomes a produced input, the act of consumption appears as an act of production, and the means of subsistence appear as costs of production. The consumption of means of subsistence produces the worker's capacity for reproducing the subsistence and also generating a net product.

The argument from subsistence places the emphasis not on the worker viewed as a person who is a particular individual with a unique set of needs associated with his personality, but on the worker as an object having so much laboring capacity with no relevant distinguishing features associated with individuality or personality.[4] This conception does not link consumption to the private life of the consumer. The worker's consumption established his place within the mass of workers, not his individuality within a society of individuals.

Individuality was restricted to those who consumed the net product and who therefore had access to wealth and luxury. Wealth and luxury remained important objectives of economic activity, but the mass of consumption (on the part of workers) only related to luxury as the means to its production.

The conception of the worker implicit in all of this emphasized the features common among workers rather than individual differences associated with personality, style of life, and mode of consumption. This emphasis on common features made possible the idea of a class of workers whose common social position dominated their wants, worldview, ideals, etc.

Early theories of the distribution of income depended heavily on the idea of a class of workers and a mode of consumption common to that class. The theories succeeded in fixing the magnitude of consumption by severing any link between consumption and the needs of the consumer for a personal life in a private sphere within which individuality could be supported and expressed.

So far, the question of what determines the magnitude and the form of subsistence needs has only been answered negatively. Since they are common to all workers, subsistence needs have nothing to do with the individual worker's personal life. What remains to determine needs once personality has been excluded from playing a role?

Some economists who worked with the idea of subsistence thought of the worker as pursuing a primitive, more or less biological, purpose in consumption. For these economists, the idea of a dominant subsistence good played an important role, at least in a symbolic sense. This good—think of it as bread or the wheat that produced the bread—constituted the stuff of life. With this stuff, a human being could sustain himself and go about whatever business his life entailed.

The idea of a stuff of life was, in its own way, a brilliant simplification. It directly eliminated any idea of choice, preference, or desire from playing a part in the most basic level of consumption. The worker's orientation toward his bread was obviously one of need and not one of preference.

But what exactly is bread? Certainly, it was as obvious to the early economist as it is to us that the bread we make from flour and water may be important to life, but it is not sufficient. Even when he leads his most elemental existence, man cannot live by bread alone.

For the early economist, the term *bread* (wheat or corn) had a symbolic meaning. It represented in a single substance the complex of life's necessities.

The introduction of the idea of subsistence accounted for the part of consumption that produced a needed input (labor) into the production of wealth. For this purpose, the idea of a stuff of life seemed unnecessarily restrictive. David Ricardo (a major figure in political economy during the early part of the nineteenth century) undertook to diversify the composition of subsistence while retaining the twin pillars of the classical conception of the economy: that subsistence was still fixed independently of the market, and that it was needed. As with much of his fundamental analysis, Karl Marx followed Ricardo's lead. But, in both cases, allowing subsistence to include a variety of different commodities introduced inconsistencies into the core of the classical idea.

Where subsistence consists of a variety of means of consumption, how can we continue to assume that its composition is fixed and necessary? The problem becomes particularly acute for Marx, who emphasizes the social and historical determinants of subsistence. Given this emphasis, what justifies the conclusion that individual desire plays no role in determining the composition of the subsistence basket? And, once we allow it to affect the composition of subsistence, can we argue with any consistency that it has no effect on its magnitude?

The implications of allowing variety in workers consumption depend on the manner in which the worker goes about assembling his subsistence. Clearly, if some individual or agency directly provides the worker with a "basket" of wages goods of fixed composition, the requirements of the classical idea continue to be met. No economist, classical or modern, has ever seriously entertained such an idea. On the contrary, in every case the worker must go to the market in pursuit of his subsistence.

Since the worker finds his subsistence in the market, he must find it by and for himself, for this is the nature of a market. Yet, for the idea of subsistence to retain its hold, the worker must direct himself and employ his initiative in finding just that basket of subsistence goods predetermined for him. This contradiction goes to the very core of the subsistence idea.

Having placed the worker in the market, we cannot expect him to allow us to dictate what he will purchase. Furthermore, if pursuit of his means of consumption leads the worker into the market, the price he must pay the seller of the products can hardly be considered irrelevant in determining the magnitude of the subsistence. The higher the prices of wages goods the smaller the basket, and the lower the prices the larger the basket. In order to retain the classical idea, we must fix both the prices of wages goods and the wage without regard to conditions of demand. Otherwise, the distribution of wealth between subsistence and luxury will depend on individual desires as they effect demand. But fixing both prices and wages in this way only leads us into conflict with the idea of wages goods acquired by the worker in the market. We can begin to see the reason for shifting from the classical idea, which is based on the premise that economic life provides the means to satisfy needs, to an altogether different idea: that economic activity is directed toward satisfaction of desires.

Our brief analysis of the classical attempt to retain necessity in economic life by using the idea of subsistence suggests two possibilities: (1) We can retain the notion of need, but only in relation to some idea of a stuff of life fixed without regard to the personality of the worker and conditions in the market; and (2) We can accept the diversity of workers' consumption, but we must allow the worker's personality to affect the composition and the price of the wages goods through its effect on demand. The latter approach implies that the structure of demand rooted in individual personality will affect the magnitude of both subsistence and net product. In the first case, we lose any meaningful notion of the worker as an individual commodity owner who acquires his means of consumption through buying and selling in markets. In the second case, we seem to lose the idea of need, and with it any possibility of finding genuine determinacy in economic life.

These two possibilities lead us to the two major schools of economic thought: the classical and the neoclassical. The classical school embraces the idea of subsistence; it does not allow individual desire to have significant impact on the course of economic affairs. The neoclassical theory emphasizes individual desire; it makes economic affairs depend on individual choices.

The subtle distinction between need and desire marks a watershed in the development of economics. Each concept expresses a basic idea about human motivation that provides the organizing principle for a whole conception. Both ideas are fundamental, yet neither seems wholly satisfying. One—need—eliminates any meaningful idea of a market economy, while the other—desire—looks on market outcomes as functions of whim and choice rather than necessity.

NEED AND PERSONALITY

The dilemma that we arrive at in thinking about how economists have understood consumer behavior originates in the underlying weakness of their ideas regarding personality. The classical theory, with its emphasis on subsistence need, eliminates the idea that individual personality has a bearing on how markets work. The modern idea of preference introduces the individual personality, but makes the individual's behavior wholly arbitrary. In order to overcome this dilemma, we need to make personality an important determinant of market outcomes without assuming that consumption decisions depend on arbitrary preferences. Our problem, in the first instance, is to root our treatment of consumption in an idea of personality that is real and determinate. We will do this by assuming that the individual personality has integrity, and that this integrity is at stake in consumption decisions.

When we say that the individual has integrity, we mean that the individual has certain qualities of personality that he wants to preserve through time. To preserve and develop these qualities requires a commitment to a way of life and an associated mode of consumption. In other words, the individual has a mode (or form) of life consistent with his personality. That mode of life defines a set of needs and acts of consumption aimed at satisfying those needs.

Integrity and mode of life express the idea that personality has a determinate structure[5] that forms itself through a process of development (the person's biography).[6] This developmental process incorporates a set of specific social relations out of which the person forms an idea of himself.[7] This idea of self motivates the individual to live his life in a way that is consistent with it. The concept of integrity refers to the internal coherence of the personality; it motivates or forces the person into a way of life. The concept of mode of life refers to a set of actions and external relations through which the specific structure of the individual's personality expresses and realizes itself.

The formation of personality through a development process constitutes a person with a sense of self or personal identity. The idea of a sense of self that motivates a mode of life makes that mode of life coherent and determinate. It also attributes a degree of necessity to the specific aspirations pursued in order to establish a mode of life. Within this context, we can speak of need as the motivation for personal consumption. Personality structure incorporates an idea of the self that requires, for its integrity to be assured, that specific needs be satisfied.

Within a mode of life, the pursuit of the means to satisfy a particular need takes on a special meaning. One need links up with another, and each particular need contributes to a structure of need that defines the mode of life. This interconnection and interdependence of needs is crucial in explaining why each individual need arises.

For example, my decision to buy a house rather than renting an apartment may be related to my passion for gardening, which I can more easily pursue if I own a house. My passion for gardening may, in turn, express my effort to define myself in relation to nature. My sense of self may involve organic gardening, a special diet excluding meat and prepared foods, and a style of life involving modes of dressing, types of entertainment, etc. Once we understand the structure as a whole, each particular element becomes intelligible. But taken by itself, a particular need makes no sense at all.

To see this, consider alternative modes of life. I may decide to buy a house rather than rent an apartment not because of an idea I have concerning my relation to nature, but because of considerations of social status (i.e., the idea I have of my place in a social hierarchy). In this case, purchasing the home has an entirely different meaning. Mere observation of an isolated act of exchange does not provide information sufficient to indicate how the good acquired provides the means to satisfy a real need. When we isolate an act of consumption or exchange we make it appear arbitrary; this drives us to think of the act in terms of whim and preference.

My passion for gardening cannot be understood outside of the mode of life that engenders it. It may, for example, express my aesthetic needs and not my need for a particular relation to nature. The evidence for the difference can be found in the overall context of a mode of life. If gardening contributes to an aesthetic meaning I give my life, then I am likely to be found attacking my land with insect sprays and chemical fertilizers, eagerly subjecting it to my aesthetic purposes. My passion for gardening links up with a wholly different mode of life involving different kinds of food, entertainment, etc.

My need for gardening may also have roots in my sense of self, since it could implicate my personal biography. I may associate gardening with a childhood experience that I can reproduce in the present through a particular activity. By reproducing this experience I also relive a relationship (for example, with a parent) that sustains my sense of self. Thus, the idea of the integrity of a sense of self requires a person to establish the coherence of a life experience. To have integrity, I must relate myself to myself by relating to my past self. This is accomplished when my mode of life simultaneously asserts my reality in the present and recalls my past, thus establishing a connection between who I was and who I am. The pursuit of biographical integrity within a mode of life has as its object assurance of the reality of the self.

The decision to have a garden means nothing unless we situate it in a structure of decisions. But once we situate the decision in this way, we make it intelligible, even inevitable. Once inevitability emerges, we have no choice but to consider decisions the result of needs. What seems at first a mere preference now appears the result of a need to sustain a mode of life that fundamentally defines the person.

If we consider the implications of our examples, the problem posed by applying of the concept of need to economic affairs comes sharply into focus. This problem has two aspects. First, we consider the aspirations of the individual to express his needs. Since need motivates the individual, his objectives are necessary to him and intelligible to us. The necessity and intelligibility of ends depend on their place within a mode of life that unifies a whole set of ends. Second, the individual remains free to pursue the means to satisfy his needs and to employ his initiative in so doing. He makes genuine decisions among the alternative available means. No one has the right to determine what he needs, and no one dictates to him the means he will acquire to satisfy his needs. He acquires the things he needs in a market environment free from coercion.

Use of the term decision may seem inconsistent with our claim that individual integrity requires acquisition of specific objects capable of satisfying determinate needs. Indeed, when it comes to consumption decisions we often find ourselves quite indecisive, and because of this we think of ourselves as making arbitrary choices. When we think this way, we lend support to the ideas of choice and preference. In order to apply the idea of need to consumer behavior, we must have an understanding of decisionmaking consistent with the idea of a personality driven by real needs. How can we reconcile our experience of indecisiveness with the idea that the integrity of our personality is at stake in consumption decisions?

Indecision can arise for two reasons.[8]   First, the outcome may not matter to us. This means that the outcome of the decision does not affect the integrity of our mode of life. We cannot decide because we have no basis for making a decision. Second, the outcome may be a matter of considerable importance and affect us deeply, but we may not know exactly how it will affect us. We may have real and important needs, but we may not know them. One important instance of this kind of indecision arises when we have conflicting needs (and conflicts within our mode of life). Indecision based on inadequate knowledge of what we need or on conflicts between opposed self-conceptions can play an important part in our lives.

When we say that we do not know what we want, or that we are torn between conflicting wants, this does not imply the absence of need. Instead, our statement implies that we do indeed want something. We may even want it quite desperately. Our problem arises either because we have a want but do not know how to satisfy it, or because our wants conflict with each other. We do not solve our problem by making an arbitrary choice based on preference, but by finding out what we do, in fact, want. When we find this out, the appearance of arbitrary choice disappears. How do I find out what I need?

If I need to, but do not know the time, or whether it is raining outside, it makes sense for me to ask someone who does. Similarly, if I want to know the price of beans or the social organization of the plantation in the antebellum south, I should find someone able to tell me. If I do not know what I want, however, this method does not work very well.

My needs are my own even when I am uncertain as to what they are. My needs are my own because they are defined within a mode of life that defines who I am. That mode of life consists of expressing, or living out, characteristics of my personal identity. My mode of life also includes the work of discovering my personal identity. To preserve my integrity as an individual, I must determine what I need. During the process of self-determination, I may be uncertain or in conflict about my mode of life and therefore about what I need. But this does not imply that I can resolve the matter by asking someone else what I need. Where needs arise out of the process of self-determination, only the individual can determine what he needs. If he does not know, he must find out for himself.

Much of life consists of the (sometimes painful) effort the individual devotes to finding out how he wants to lead his life and therefore what he really needs. During this process, mistakes are made. The individual fails to satisfy needs he does have while working hard to satisfy needs he does not have. Furthermore, when needs conflict and the individual satisfies one, he thereby fails to satisfy another. As a result, the individual experiences confusion and frustration, which can lead to indecision. This indecision does not mean that individuals have no needs, or that they make arbitrary choices rather than decisions based on necessity. It does mean that the individual must be the authority on the requirements of his mode of life. Because of this, the individual must decide between alternatives, and the decision must be truly his. In this sense, the individual remains free to decide for himself. But what he decides on is what he really needs.

The individual's biography consists of a long process of discovery or self-seeking. Through this process, the individual defines and develops a mode of life that incorporates an idea of personal identity or sense of self. The importance of the market for the individual stems from the way in which it both allows and requires him to discover and define his own way of life.

Two seemingly inconsistent requirements must be met in developing a conception of the market based on the idea of need. First, in pursuing the means to satisfy his needs, the individual is driven by necessity—the necessity of sustaining a mode of life synonymous with his very identity. Second, in pursuing the means to satisfy his needs, the individual is "free to choose."

Both elements play decisive roles in our economic and social lives. In the market we are free to buy or not buy a commodity (assuming, of course, that we have the purchasing power), but we also need the commodities we purchase. It is important that no one forces us to buy the things we buy even though we buy them because we need them and have no other way of acquiring them. Our integrity may depend on acquiring an object necessary to the sustenance of a mode of life, and our integrity may equally depend on our right to determine for ourselves just what objects are essential to that mode of life. This right affects our whole orientation toward our economic lives. It affects how we view ourselves, and since what we need depends on how we see ourselves, it also affects what we buy and sell.

Thus, I buy a house because I need it; but for the house to express my personality, buying it must be my decision. If someone were to give me the house or force me to buy it, ownership of the house would express *their* will and sense of self. Even though I formally owned it, I would be living in someone else's house, not my own. Since I express myself through my property, I need that property; but acquisition of the property must be a freely undertaken act. This peculiar unity of freedom and necessity profoundly affects the need and the means to satisfying it.

Consider the need for transportation. I can satisfy my need to move from one place to another in different ways. How I get from place to place depends on my mode of transportation. When I drive a car, I transport myself. Ownership of a car allows me to control my mode of transportation in a unique way. I determine the pace, the route, and the time of departure. Style also enters into consideration. When I transport myself, I may be bold or timid, enthusiastic or bored, taciturn or gregarious. My need to move from one place to another has all of these aspects; and the mode of transportation I employ should have the appropriate range of qualities to satisfy my multifaceted need.

Among alternative modes of transportation, the automobile stands out in two ways. First, as a mode of self-transportation it satisfies a need for autonomy and self-determination. Second, as personal property the automobile can be adapted to its owner's personality. Unlike trains, planes, and buses, which must satisfy simultaneously the needs of large numbers of different individuals and therefore ignore individual qualities of customers, automobiles can be adapted to particular owners. I can acquire a car with a specific combination of features (style, size, color, etc.) appropriate to my personality.

The use of a car responds to the individual's need for self-determination. Both object (car) and need (transportation) are saturated with the ideas of individual autonomy and private consumption. Without a car I suffer a failure of autonomy, and a diminution of my person. To this extent, I need a car if I am to become the person I envision myself to be. This dependence stands in sharp contrast to the idea that I may merely prefer owning a car to taking the bus.

The fact that a car is my personal property plays a major part in my need for it. When my mode of transportation is my property, it can help to support my self-expression and self-determination. The link between ownership and autonomy suggests a link between private needs and the market. This link involves my participating in the acquisition of what I need in a particular way: I must be free to acquire those things that I decide I need. The element of self-determination governs the kinds of needs which I have, the kinds of things that satisfy those needs, and the way in which I go about acquiring those things (e.g., exchange). So long as my freedom and self-determination must be expressed through my mode of life and mode of consumption, I have a need for my means of consumption. The decisions I make about what I need express the fundamental character of my needs.

My sense of who I am drives me to activities designed to express, assert, and realize my personal identity. Through these activities I first acquire the means to satisfy my needs, and then by consuming those means fulfill the associated needs. In this respect, I must not think of my sense of self as passive, inert, or fixed. I must treat it as a goal to be achieved, a potential to be realized, a reality to be asserted and made objective through my actions. My sense of self is an idea (also an ideal) I have of who I am; it is this idea that drives me into action.

This result brings us one step closer to isolating the force of necessity that drives the individual to articulate and attempt to satisfy a set of peculiarly human needs. When we say that a fish needs the sea, we do not mean that the fish has a sense of self that is diminished or destroyed when it is removed from the water. Instead, we imply a kind of coercion, the presence of a power the individual fish cannot resist. The idea of need connotes this power over the individual. In the case of human needs, this power operates through what we have called a sense of self.

Thus far, we have considered only those needs that people satisfy by consuming goods. Among other things, this leaves out the way in which a person's role in production determines his particular needs and gives expression to his self-conception. When a person's work helps to realize a sense of self, we say that the person has a vocation.

When I have a vocation, I am deeply invested in my life's work; I make no sharp distinction between who I am and what I do. This quality of work appears most vividly for those individuals who have a professional identity that makes them, for example, an artist, a scholar, or a doctor. But the idea of a vocation has wide applicability, since one's personality may be appropriate or inappropriate to driving a truck or taxi, waiting on tables, or cutting hair. Does this mean that while different vocations fit different personalities, all vocations are appropriate to the expression of personality and sense of self?

In order to answer this question, we need to consider the relation between vocation and personality more closely. While a vocation can give expression to a sense of self and by so doing support the development and realization of personality, commitment to a vocation can also impede the process of self-development. Conflict can arise in two cases: (1) when the vocation so absorbs the person's whole life that he loses the ability to distinguish between work and self, and (2) when work does not provide an avenue for the expression of self.

Part of the danger a vocation poses to personality has to do with time. The greater the proportion of a person's life taken over by work, the stronger the identification between the person and his work. The stronger this identification, the greater the likelihood that the person will disappear into his work. When this happens we have vocational or work identity but not personal or individual identity. The distinctiveness and unique attributes of personality and of personal biography have little opportunity to develop. As a result, when we adopt life-absorbing vocations we seriously weaken the distinctively individual attributes of our personalities.

Contemporary ways of life tend to make personal identity increasingly independent of vocation. Since we also develop and express ourselves outside our vocations, who we are cannot be reduced to the work we do. While all accountants may be similar in certain respects, each individual accountant also strives to be a distinctive person, irreducible to the generic accountant. Not only does this take time (and take time away from work), it also makes the person independent (to a degree) from work. Thus, our persons preceed our vocations. We express this important idea when we say that a person must be allowed (and enabled) to choose a vocation.

In some societies, people are born to particular social positions, including particular work responsibilities. Since people are born to their vocations, their personalities (so far as that term is applicable) must adapt to pre-determined work identities. By contrast, in modern society people seek out their vocations. This requires individuals to make judgments about what sort of work will best realize their sense of self. It also requires individuals to make certain that work allows the expression of personality both during work time and outside.

The condition that individuals involve themselves in determining their vocations limits the set of vocations appropriate to them. While vocation can play an important part in the expression of personality, outside of this set it poses a threat to the person's establishment of a distinctive identity. The danger arises when work absorbs life even though the work itself provides scope for the expression of personality. Certain kinds of work pose an even greater threat because they do not provide any opportunity for self-expression. We use the term labor to connote the kind of work that, because of its essentially routinized or mechanical quality, does not contribute to the person's sense of self.

When we labor we treat our bodies and minds as objects. When we treat our bodies and minds as objects we treat ourselves as a means to achieving an external goal. We do labor in the purest sense when our goal has nothing directly to do with our sense of self. When this kind of labor comprises our life's work, our vocation does not allow us to express ourselves, and in this narrower sense we do not have a true vocation.

Wage labor provides the classic example of work that is not a vocation. Because it is labor it does not directly allow us to express ourselves. Because we do it for money—wages—its actual product is not our actual goal. As a result of this, we can speak of the wage laborer as alienated from himself and his product. What we mean is that the activity and its product are unconnected to the personality of the worker. I have considered these implications of wage labor in greater detail elsewhere (Levine 1978, Chap. 7, and 1981, Chap. 7). The point to emphasize here is the implication of wage labor for the relation of personality to vocation. The presence of labor as the life work for members of society demands a negative answer to our question concerning the appropriateness of all work to personality development. The relation of personality to vocation significantly restricts the idea of appropriate vocation.

This restriction has important implications for the traditional notion of class structure. When we think of a working class we have in mind a social group distinguished by its work—wage labor—work that is not a vocation. This lack of vocation, together with the idea of subsistence, makes the needs of class membership stand in place of the needs of the individual. When we treat persons as members of such a class we abstract from or even deny the existence of their need for a personalized mode of consumption and for a vocation through which they can achieve a degree of self-realization.

The idea of a working class exemplifies the second of the two cases identified earlier of conflict between work and self-development. The idea of a capitalist class exemplifies the other case. We will consider the vocation of the capitalist and its relation to self-realization in Chapter 5. Until then, we will treat vocation as a part of a person's mode of life, and therefore as a vehicle for the realization of the individual's sense of self.

The idea of need has importance, then, in thinking both about consumption and about work. To summarize our argument up to this point: The necessity of a particular need stems from its location within a structure of needs. The necessity of the structure as a whole stems from the form of life that defines it. This form of life expresses and realizes the individual's personal identity and sense of self. The driving force behind my form of life is an idea I have of who I am, an idea I assert and realize through work and consumption.

I may see myself as hardworking, frugal, austere, and morally upright. The effort to conform to the ideas I have about myself governs my life. These ideas, together with my personal biography and the various related attributes I strive to see in myself, determine what I need. If I see myself as a classical scholar, then this sense of self dictates my "taste" in food, clothing, entertainment, etc. None of this implies that every classical scholar has the same taste. No individual identity can be reduced to the idea "classical scholar," and that idea also manifests itself in different ways. The idea I have of myself is very complex, even contradictory. Furthermore, I may be governed by such an idea without being fully aware of it. Nonetheless, my aspirations can always be made intelligible if I can discover the ideas that drive them.

When I order my life according to the idea I have of who I am, I define a set of peculiarly human needs that are genuine requirements of life. But, how can the idea which I have of myself involve a power over me?

Needs connected to personality are peculiar in that the individual asserts them and acts as their source. In this sense, their power originates within the individual. At the same time, the power needs have over the individual implies that their origin cannot be wholly internal. The power of need must have its origin both within and outside the individual. Where do my needs come from? Or, equivalently, what is the source of the idea I have of myself that orders my life?

The necessity of human need requires it to be in some sense objective—it must have a reality that is not wholly contingent on private whims. The reality of a material thing is objective in just this sense. The existence of the tree in my yard does not depend on my personal perception of that tree. If I perceive a purple rhinoceros in my yard, but this perception is mine alone, then we would say that this rhinoceros does not really exist (i.e., exists only in my imagination, not in reality). The rhinoceros lacks objectivity.

Human needs derive their force from an idea (the sense of self that defines a mode of life). The reality of this idea also depends on its objectivity. For this reason, we can speak of "realizing" (living out through acts of work and consumption) or "expressing" (communicating to others) who we are. For there to be peculiarly human needs, the idea that we have about who we are must be objective; otherwise it would have no power over us. But, what makes this idea objective or real? It turns out that the objective reality of a sense of self depends on its social meaning. In effect, I find my personal identity in society since only society can define (or give meaning to) a mode of life.[9]

By dressing in a particular way, I express something important about my personality. A three-piece suit expresses a sense of style and position in society different from that expressed by a flannel shirt and a pair of overalls. But, in both cases my dress meaningfully conveys a sense of self. Were I to walk into a room dressed in either way, I would communicate something about the way in which I perceive myself. When I communicate my idea of self to others, this helps to make my idea real and objective.

If I were to enter a room encased in a bullet-shaped metal container, the result would be decidely different. Those in the room would not understand the idea of self expressed in this way and the only meaning I would succeed in conveying would be one of personality disorder. In this case, my perception of self remains personal. As such, it has no reality outside of me; for others it remains unreal. But if I fail to establish the reality of my idea for others, its reality for me is placed on the shakiest foundation. The purpose of entering of a room in a metal container continues to be that of making my sense of self objective. The puzzled looks and derisive comments leave me frustrated in my objective, and doubtful about my own reality.

Thus, to make my idea of myself objective and real I must share it with others. This takes us to a decisive point in our investigation of human need: the specification of the world outside of the individual to which he has recourse when he seeks to discover the idea according to which he will order his life. Once we know where the individual looks for his identity, we will know something about the nature of the individual's sense of self, and this will provide important information about the kinds of needs appropriate to economic activities, especially the market.

The sustenance and definition of my individual personality depends on its social recognition. When my mode of life has a social meaning, the attributes of my personality become objective—not only to others, but also for me. Thus, self-seeking drives me into social relations.

When we speak of the way in which social recognition makes individual identity objective, we are not referring exclusively to recognition on the part of other people. Were my identity contingent on its recognition by some particular individual, it would be no more objective than when I alone perceive it. The social meaning is crucial. When I purchase a particular kind of car, I may do so because of a need to identity myself with the social meaning associated with that car. Different cars have different meanings and fit into different modes of life. In a real sense, the social meaning attaches to the car; it is an objective attribute of the car and potentially of its owner regardless of who, if anyone, sees the owner driving the car. Particular persons do not create social meaning; social meanings create (or make up the identities of) particular persons.

In order to establish my individuality and autonomy, I must make myself the source of my mode of life and associated needs. But the material out of which I build my identity consists of meanings socially defined and created. My individual personality is a uniquely constructed mozaic of socially defined needs. I do the work of construction by combining and sometimes modifying social meanings in my own individual way. The result, when successful, realizes the idea I have of myself as simultaneously individual/personal and social. This is the self-determination of the individual as a social construct.

In this sense, individual needs are social needs, needs that are made objective and real by their social meaning. Since recognizability makes my identity real, self-seeking defines a set of needs or requirements of life that, while social, also have their source in my individual personality. When I pursue the means to the satisfaction of my needs, I act as an autonomous agent whose needs originate in me. For this reason, the market seems an appealing environment in which I might find the things I need.

It may be the case that only certain ideas are appropriate for ordering the lives of persons. We also need to consider what it means for ideas to be appropriate in this sense. One important way in which society limits possible ways of life involves appeal to ethical or moral considerations. When society appeals to moral considerations, it sometimes places severe limits on ways of life. For the present, we will not attempt to consider the social construction of ways of life on the basis of moral considerations. We will focus instead on aspects of the social meaning of modes of life for which the ethical component remains implicit.

SOCIAL NEED

A social need arises out of the individual's efforts to order his life according to an idea whose reality depends on its social meaning. If we define social need exclusively in this way, however, our definition seems largely formal. The definition refers directly to the way in which we establish the reality of our need (exclusively in society), but it makes no reference to the kind of need that becomes real through its social recognition. What limits exist on the kinds of ideas that can achieve social recognition? In order to develop a more substantial conception of social need, we must also consider the content of the ideas that order our lives in society.

If I strive to order my life according to the idea of a tree, I attempt to live the life of a tree by satisfying tree-like needs. A person who strives to be tree, however, not only makes a very poor showing as a tree, but also makes a poor showing as a person. Indeed, whatever remnants of humanity I continue to exhibit in my tree-like behavior will be found in the ways in which I fail in my aspiration to live the life of a tree.

Although it may be less immediately apparent, the same result holds when I attempt to organize my life according to my conception of the natural imperatives of my own species. Close inspection of the way in which we apply the term "natural" to a mode of life quickly reveals the peculiar implications of the idea that an individual's sense of self can be defined by a series of species imperatives.

In common usage, the idea of a natural way of life does not connote adherence to the imperatives of the species as it would exist in nature. "Natural food," for example, bears no significant connection to what people ate in nature before civilization. Similarly, the state of "physical fitness" has few roots in the condition of the human body prior to the development of civilization and culture.

On the contrary, "natural food" and "physical fitness" are ideas we have about ourselves; they are parts of ways of life in society capable of providing elements of our recognition as particular kinds of persons. As such, they only make sense in society, and the needs associated with them are social needs. Thus, the idea of a "natural" style of life embodies a paradox. This paradox stems from its social nature and the implied separation of the individual committed to the natural lifestyle from nature.

Unlike true species imperatives, the specific needs that arise in our efforts to be "fit" and lead a "natural" lifestyle help to distinguish our modes of life from those of others. True species imperatives must, by their nature, be common to all members of the species. Thus, I can achieve social recognition for qualities of my personality when I organize my life according to society's idea of what is natural. But to do so is the antithesis of ordering my life according to the true imperatives of man in nature.

There is no more certain way of losing your humanity than by organizing your life exclusively or primarily with species imperatives. Such imperatives assert themselves independently of the ideas we have about ourselves. Indeed we do not think at all before we act instinctually. When we think about what we do, our reason for acting does not stem from the biological imperatives of the species. Explanation of our action requires an explicit account of the content of the thinking that preceeds and occurs simultaneously with the action. Our ideas about our place in society make up the content of the thought processes that organize and direct us when we work and consume. As we have seen, these ideas have a social determination. But social recognition and construction of actions through thought only make sense if the ideas and the activities have a meaning or purpose distinct from the attainment of the biological needs of the species. This purpose arises out of imperatives individuals experience only as members of a social order. Imperatives of individuation have this quality; they define needs associated with being an individual within a society of individuals.

In modern society, each person has his own individual needs. The needs associated with distinguishing one person from another provide specific content for the social determination of the individual. They are imperatives independent of biological life. For the species in nature, individuality is irrelevant. Biological needs are held in common. While this is true of some social needs, social needs also differ for each individual.

We satisfy some of our needs by consuming goods. The idea of an individual need implies that a social purpose determines the act of consumption. Yet the actual consumption of a particular good normally has physical and physiological as well as social aspects. Would it not be more sensible to think about the acts of consumption made possible by our participation in the economy as having both social and natural determinants? We could then think about the economy as a system of relations directed toward provisioning needs regardless of whether those needs originate in social or natural imperatives.

Consider the activity of eating breakfast. Hunger, in the primal biological sense, may certainly play a role in sending us to the breakfast table. We may also, however, experience hunger in a purely social sense. Our need may be for building a strong body, or leading a "natural" life. Such needs are fulfilled when we consume a breakfast cereal we believe is appropriate to these needs. Alternatively, we may not be hungry in a biological sense at all, but we may experience food as a surrogate for the affection we do not receive in more direct and adequate forms. We may think we are hungry for nutrients, when we really hunger for a social relation.[10]

Eating breakfast, considered as an event occurring in time and space, can involve all of these aspects. To describe such an event requires reference to the simultaneous pursuit and satisfaction of natural and social (including psychological) needs. Does it follow that all those determinants relevant to describing the event as it occurs in time and space also contribute to determining its economic purpose? If we grant that in consuming breakfast we experience a physiological process that helps to satisfy a biological need, must we also grant that the biological need helps to account for the economic activities leading up to the consumption act—specifically the production, marketing, and sale of the breakfast cereal?

If we ask why introduce a market for the provisioning of needs, our answer requires a specification of the kinds of needs satisfied by objects that the market provides.[11] The distinctive purpose of the market is its special ability to provide means of consumption that meet the needs of the individual to be an individual. Markets make sense when individual initiative is part of the work of need satisfaction. If we want to understand the work markets do in society, we are not aided by references to biological reproduction. If biological reproduction is our sole or even primary end, markets are unnecessary. Such reproduction can be, and normally is, accomplished without buying and selling. The "fact" that consuming products of economic activity helps assure our biological sustenance in no way establishes a biological determination of the needs that drive us into economic affairs.

Indeed, markets are notorious for providing food that not only lacks nutritional value, but is positively harmful to the biological life of the consumer. Even those foods that do provide nutrition have, until recently, been advertised on the basis of virtues other than nutrition (e.g., taste, cost, convenience). The educated consumer who concerns himself with the nutritional value of the food he acquires in the market provides no counterargument. As we have seen, his purpose is not biological survival, but the attainment of a socially defined ideal. The balanced diet that he strives to attain has little to do with the biological imperatives of the survival of the species in its natural state; as a rule, they are in excess of what the species survived on in that state. The very idea of species survival (length of life, state of health, etc.) has an entirely new meaning in society.

The distinctive purpose of the market is not biological sustenance, but support of the social being of the individual. This conclusion suggests an important problem that is a core concern of political economy: Is the market the appropriate institution for providing people with the means to satisfy organic needs defined by physiological drives? As we will see later, one of the defining characteristics of a private enterprise system is the requirement that people depend on the market for the satisfaction of virtually all of their needs (social and physiological). This naturally implies that there is significant inequality in the ability of people to realize their sense of self through the acquisition of the things needed to support their modes of life. Thus, if I have a low income but a significant need for medical care, and if I must use my income to pay for medical care, then my ability to realize a meaningful mode of life in society suffers and the integrity of my person may be seriously harmed. If health care is an example of a physiological need that does not involve the assertion of my identity as a particular individual, and if the social purpose of the market is to facilitate the pursuit of individual modes of life, then providing health care through the market can impede the market from accomplishing its real purpose. In such cases, it is important to restrict the market to providing the means to satisfy those needs specifically connected to individual self-determination.

NEED AND IMPULSE

Thus far our argument for rooting consumption decisions in need leaves no room for the exercise of preferences. Because of this, the resulting conception may appear rigid and implausible if we intend it as a general account of the motivations standing behind economic life. Presumably, individuals understand many of their own decisions as an effort to satisfy a desire, or even a whim. To be sure, when the individual acts in accord with what he thinks is unconstrained desire, he may in fact be following a rigidly prescribed path. This is implied by the Freudian interpretation of mental life. Psychoanalytic theory interprets the apparently trivial decisions of everyday life on the basis of underlying psychic processes that are not arbitrary or capricious. This means that our interpretation of our own act as resulting from a whim does not in itself deny the existence of a need. As it turns out, a more complex interpretation of desire (or preference) need not conflict with the foregoing treatment of decisionmaking based on needs connected to individual integrity.

Nonetheless, we should not ignore the way the individual himself interprets his decisions, even when he interprets them as whim and preference. The distinction we make in daily life between needs and preferences may be more complex than we think it is so that the underlying reality may conflict with our understanding of it. Yet our interpretation has its own force, and the distinction it insists on has implications for how we act and how we arrive at our decisions. Our problem, then, is to develop an understanding of those decisions involving the exercise of preference (or desire) that treats preference on the basis of the notions of personal integrity and need.

The idea that we make decisions about ourselves without deliberation contributes to our sense of individual freedom and self-determination. One way in which we characterize ourselves when we accede to our desires in this way is to say that we yield to impulse. The term impulse expresses a complex relation between freedom and determination. We identify freedom with yielding to our impulses or inclinations; yet, when we yield to impulse we lose control over our lives. Thus the act that expresses our freedom also negates it. This happens because yielding to impulse does not free us from determination; it only frees us from the process of deliberation through which we come to know how we are determined.

The distinction between preference and need involves how we know the reason for our action. While we think of this difference quantitatively—need has more force than preference—and indeed our needs drive us harder and further than our preferences, the difference is fundamentally qualitative. Our need seems stronger in part because its foundation or reason is more transparent. It is clear that I need a car in order to travel to a well-defined destination (e.g., to work). I know why I have this need, and I may even use the term need only for relations with explicit and well-defined objectives. I may also be reasonably aware that I need a particular type of car that expresses explicitly understood aspects of my personality. But why do I need my car to be of this particular make or this particular color? The difference between the two types of need is that one compels more forcefully than the other (I must have a particular kind of car, but I might settle for a less satisfactory color), and that one appears directly in relation to reasons while the other does not. We need to emphasize that the distinction between need and impulse cannot be drawn for the object by itself but depends on the part it plays in the life of the consumer. Thus, color can be a matter of necessity for me while for someone else acquisition of a car itself may be done on impulse.

The relation of need to preference requires us to distinguish decisions based on deliberation and explicit reasons from decisions based on hidden reasons and the absense of deliberation. We use the term impulse to refer to needs that we feel but do not know. The kind of society we live in is dependent on the scope we allow for impulse. If that scope is too narrow, our sense of our freedom erodes; if it is too great, we become impulse-driven agents subject to irrational forces and the influence of others. In this second case, by yielding to impulse we give up our self-determination.

Self-determination requires that we know who we are; and if we do, we also know why we have particular needs. This means that we cannot be free if the whole, or greater part of, our lives is governed by impulse. But freedom also involves us in a denial of our neediness. This denial takes place when we make decisions by yielding to impulse.

In the remainder of our analysis, we focus on need because it underlies impulse and because it is the core concept that distinguishes our conception from the classical and the neoclassical. We will refer to this distinction between need and preference where relevant and consider some of its implications for economic relations.

NEED AND RIGHT

In a well-developed market society, when we establish that we need something in order to support our integrity, we sometimes also conclude that our need places an obligation on society. If I have a need, does this obligate society to provide me with an object capable of satisfying that need? When does the individual have a right to the things he needs?

If the individual has such a right, then the distribution of wealth must be restricted in such a way so as to assure that he can acquire what he needs. In effect, an affirmative answer to this question entails the idea of a just distribution of wealth, since justice results from due respect for rights.[12] For us, however, the really fundamental question is not that of the particular form a just distribution of wealth would take. Before considering the ethical properties of alternative distributions of wealth, we must first resolve the following question: Do the concepts of justice and rights have any relevance to the distribution of income and wealth among persons?[13]

As we will see later, within a private enterprise economy, the specification of property rights severely restricts questions about the justice of patterns of property ownership. If we accept the implications of a private enterprise system, the issue of justice will apply only to the method by which individuals acquire wealth—exchange—and not to the amount of wealth they acquire. The specific distribution of wealth that results from free exchange is not, in itself, either just or unjust.[14] So long as wealth is acquired without violating the principle of freedom of exchange (i.e., without violating the property rights of the participants), its ownership, in whatever amount, is just.

Acceptance of the implications of a private enterprise system militates against any consistent argument in support of even such limited rights to wealth as those implied in the ideas of social welfare, national health insurance, the minimum wage, etc. Economists who favor adoption of such policies within the context of private enterprise tend to do so on the basis of appeal to values rather than rights. As a result, movement toward what is perceived to be a more equitable distribution takes the form of charity rather than the recognition of the rights of the individual to some proportional part of social wealth.

Without a reasoned appeal to rights, however, it is difficult to evaluate the justice of a pattern of wealth distribution. And, if we do not invoke the idea of justice as a basis for ethical claims regarding wealth distribution, we can hardly avoid injustice and wrongful appropriation. So far as economic affairs are concerned, the idea of a just society must involve an explicit and reasoned judgment regarding our two questions: Does the idea of justice apply to the distribution of wealth? And, if it does, what rights do we have to receive and acquire the means for satisfying our needs?

Before considering the relevance of justice to wealth distribution, we first need to make more explicit some implications of the idea of right. This would not be problematic if we restricted ourselves to a particular society within which rights take definite form in relation to law and social practice. To some extent, we will do just this. Insofar as our notion of right conforms to its meaning and use in modern society, it gains determinacy from its relation to a prevailing social order. But insofar as our concept of right deviates, as it will at certain points, from the prevailing notion of right in modern society, we must presuppose a standard of judgment more universal than that which supports a determination of right based on prevailing practice. This means that our concept of right must be theoretically grounded. In this book we presuppose this grounding rather than developing it explicitly. In order to make the nature of this presupposition clearer, we will indicate briefly what lies at the core of the theory.

The core of our underlying theory of right is the relationship between the idea that personality has integrity and the requirement that the integrity of the person emerge out of a process of self-discovery and self-determination. The crucial implication drawn out by the theory is that integrity of the person requires respect for others—that my integrity can only be realized if the idea of respect for the integrity of others constitutes an element of my personality structure. This approach to the theory of right combines the idea of personality structure developed in the twentieth century on the basis of the work of Freud with the abstract idea of the person developed in the eighteenth and nineteenth centuries by Kant and Hegel. Given this theoretical context, the term right will normally carry with it the implications of an attribute of persons. To be a person means to have the capacity for certain rights so that all those, and only those, who are fully persons must have all their rights respected. Our theory of rights excludes the possibility that rights can be distributed nonuniformly among persons.

Since our underlying theory of right incorporates respect for the integrity of others as a central concern, it has an affinity with modern versions of contractualist moral theory.[15] Our theory differs from that tradition primarily in its emphasis on personality structure. A theory of right that takes the concrete requirements of the self-determination of persons into account should have some distinctive implications even if it accepts fundamental notions such as the priority of justice over utility and the necessity of considering the standpoint of the person in abstraction from particular needs.[16]

Rights designate arenas within which action is contingent on the person's will. Property rights provide persons with discretion in the use and general disposition of a specific set of objects. In this respect, property right designates a realm for the exercise of will, a set of actions that are, in the most fundamental sense up, to the person. The same result holds for other rights, such as those to life and to privacy.

When I have a right over some object or activity, this means that I determine the activity and the manner of the object's disposal. In this sense, my right endows me with power. Yet my right to act does not stem from my power to do so. I may have power due to physical strength, financial resources, knowledge, or personal influence, but this power does not provide me with the right to act.

For my action to be rightful, its legitimacy must be recognized. In this sense, when I have a right I have the authority to act. Right and authority to act are not, however, synonymous. The kind of authority associated with right is distinctive because it makes the actor the source of his authority. I have a right to act when my power to do so is recognized by others to be innate to me without regard to my physical, intellectual, or financial resources, and without regard to my official position in society.

When a policeman arrests a criminal, his authority to do so comes not from him but from the law and from the designation of his position as an agent of the law responsible for its enforcement. When I have a right the authority stems not from the law, but from my person. We make this same point when we say that rights are innate to persons. Because I am a citizen, I have certain rights. No higher authority gives me those rights or has the authority to take them away.

The idea that rights are innate is captured in the principle of equal treatment before the law.[17] The principle of equal treatment says something important about the way in which rights are, so to speak, distributed among persons. The principle asserts that all those who have rights have the same rights, and in equal measure. Rights are universal in the sense that they apply to all persons equally. No one has rights that are peculiarly theirs. The principle has not, however, been applied to the economy, and particularly to the problem of the distribution of wealth. We do not apply this principle to the distribution of wealth as a result of our commitment to the institution of private enterprise. Equal treatment (or what we will later term equal regard) applied to the distribution of wealth conflicts with the right of the individual to devote himself to the work of accumulating wealth. When individuals devote themselves to becoming wealthy, they necessarily contribute to the creation of differences between persons in wealth and status. In Chapter 5 and in the epilogue, we will consider some implications of applying the principle of equal treatment to the distribution of wealth.

When I exercise my property right, I dispose of items that I own. If I own a car, then the prevailing idea of property right applies to my car. But, I have no particular right to my car, additional to my right to own property. The rights themselves do not include any specification of the actions that I will take in their name. Since rights do not specify the particular action taken in their name, they have no connection to particular features of my personality (e.g., my needs). My endowment of rights does not depend on those elements of my personality that distinguish me from others. I am endowed with rights because I am a person just like others.

If different people have authority in different areas, then their authority cannot stem from their being persons, but from outside. If

I have property, but there are others who cannot own property, then either (1) I am a person while others are not, or (2) property ownership is not a right but a privilege bestowed on me by a higher authority. In the first case, I retain property rights because the source of my authority over my possessions is in my person. In the second case, however, I am more the custodian than the owner of the property. Thus, for me to claim a right, I must claim that my authority comes not simply from my person, but from my being a person.[18] For this claim to make sense, I must see rights as attributes of being a person. Since possession of rights helps to define who is fully a person, rights are said to be inalienable; to give them up is to become less than a person.

For me to be a person, I must assert my will in the world, or act on the basis of my own initiative. I cannot allow my behavior to depend on instinct or the will of others. Doing so makes me an object to others and less than a person. Particular rights designate those kinds of actions subject to the will and initiative of the person. In this sense, our specification of particular rights depends on the idea we have of what it means to be a person.

Thus far in our treatment of the individual, we have emphasized the importance of expressing individual personality within socially recognized modes of life. We have argued that attributes of individual personality only exist when they have social meaning and can be expressed in relations between persons. The specification of particular rights depends heavily on this result.

We will assume that rights have meaning and significance for us because of the part they play in establishing and expressing our social being. In the case of property rights, they express our individuality. Thus, property rights are innate and inalienable so far as the ability of the individual to exert his will over a set of objects is necessary to his social recognition as a person. If individual personality can sustain, realize, and express itself without ownership over property, then the idea of property rights loses its signficance. If property ownership is unnecessary to the life of the individual in society, no strong argument exists to protect property rights, regardless of whether such rights are protected by law.[19]

We can think about certain of our other rights in this same way. As we have seen, to be an individual, I must have an idea of myself, and I must be able to gain the social recognition of my idea through my actions. My right to express my ideas through speaking and writing stems in part from the dependence of my personality upon ideas that I strive to "live up to." To realize myself, I must be able to convey to others, in actions and in words, these ideas of mine, which establish who I am.[20] This right may also stem in part from the requirements of political life. In this case the link between rights and personality depends on the way in which to be a person I must also participate in a political order and view the public interest as my own end.

Property rights and the right to freedom of expression are necessary if we are to adequately express personalities. Given this link between rights and the idea of a person,[21] how can we answer our original question concerning the relation of rights to needs? Does access to the things I need constitute one of my rights?

If property rights are recognized and if I happen to own something I need, then I have a right to use it so as to satisfy my need. If, however, I do not own an object I need, and yet I have a right to satisfy my need, then a measure of property right follows from need. Our question concerns the way in which right follows need, if it does at all.

It is clear that when we employ the idea of preference, the issue of right becomes moot. The term preference has relevance only when a person's integrity does not depend on the acquisition of objects he desires. Since a person does not require access to such objects, he has no right to them stemming from the demands of personhood.

The notion of preference will not support the idea of a right to, or a just distribution of, wealth. By contrast, the individual's attitude toward his needs makes possible the idea that the individual may have rights to some manner and degree of need satisfaction. (It is too early to determine whether even the concept of need supports such rights). The concept of social need places the question of a just distribution of wealth on the agenda; the concept of preference does not.

Given our special concern here with individual needs, however, it is still difficult to see how the individual could have a right to an object that would satisfy his need. As we have seen, any right I have, I must recognize equally in all other persons. Yet the distinctiveness of my needs stems precisely from their connection to the unique qualities of my personality. I cannot recognize my needs equally in all other persons and still retain my individuality. Thus, how can I claim a special right over those particular objects that satisfy my needs?

If a starving man needs an apple I own, then even though I do not need the apple myself, he has no right to it stemming from his need. Much depends on whether someone else owns the object the individual needs. Even if in some sense the starving man has a right to some means of sustenance, it does not follow that he has any right to my property.

If I do not need the apple and put it up for sale, and if the person who needs it has the means to purchase it, we may want to argue that he has a right to purchase the apple from me. My property right may not include the right to refuse to sell an object to someone assuming that I am prepared to sell it to someone else. The question then becomes: Does the individual have a right to means of purchase "adequate" to satisfy his needs?

This is a more satisfactory question since it at least makes sense to think of a measure of wealth being necessary to sustain the individual regardless of his particular needs and personality. Insofar as a market economy separates to a degree the distribution of money wealth from the distribution of means of consumption, it makes possible a right to wealth needed to satisfy particular needs but not defined by the personal needs of individuals. As we explore the idea of wealth, we will focus more closely on an answer to the question raised in this section concerning its just distribution.

WEALTH 2

UTILITY

When we consume a good with the purpose of satisfying our needs, we make use of it. Thus, the notion of use specifies a certain kind of consumption: one whose end is the satisfaction of need. When a fire consumes a warehouse, we do not say that the fire has used up the warehouse. But, after years of service as a place of storage, the warehouse may very well be used up. Use, then, is a particular way of relating to an object. But what of the object we use? What makes something a "useful object?" In particular, does the consumer determine the object's use according to his subjective desire, or does the object in some sense tell us how we must use it?

Here, we can again consider two alternatives. First, we can place the entire burden on the side of the consumer. We do this when we make the object's utility primarily a matter of the subjective desires of the consumer. In this case, the consumer determines (1) whether the object is useful; (2) how useful it is; and (3) what specific use it has. Second, we can think of the object as having an intrinsic use or set of uses determined independently of the consumer's desires. This makes utility objective.

The subjective notion of utility works well with the ideas of preference and choice since it emphasizes the individual's freedom to use the object however he sees fit. It allows the same utility, or subjective satisfaction, to be derived from different objects. The idea of an "indifference" curve plotting different combinations of objects capable of providing the same utility captures the idea that the consumer determines the utility of the object for himself, and that utility connotes the purely subjective attitude of the individual toward the object.

Subjective utility allows us to measure usefulness in a particular way, because it makes all objects commensurate in the minds of their owners or prospective owners. We measure objects by their degree of usefulness to us, which reflects the intensity of our desire for them.

The objective notion of utility works well with our idea of need. The importance we attribute to establishing the objectivity of individual needs is well served by objects whose utility is defined for us, and whose use by us provides directly for social recognition because that use is not contingent on our personal preferences.

Consider the utility of a desk. From the subjective standpoint, the crucial question concerns the individual's intensity of desire. In other words, we focus on the state of mind of the individual sitting behind the desk (or the individual who anticipates sitting behind the desk). In effect, the idea of specific use has been suppressed. The term "desk" used to describe the object does not imply any constraint on its utility to its owner.

We cannot help but notice that this makes for a very odd notion of use. Normally, a desk is a desk regardless of how much or how little an individual desires it. You cannot drive to work or eat it for dinner. To be sure, there may be a range of things you can do with it, but they are all contained in the notion of a desk. Even when we fail to find anyone who wants to use a particular desk, we continue to recognize it as a desk.

The notion of objective utility captures this meaning. It makes the intensity of my desire for the desk not a part of its utility, but only of my personal attitude towards it. The utility of the desk has been defined for me, so that when I use it I fulfill a destiny built into the desk.

The objective notion allows me to think of utility quantitatively, and the relevant measures have nothing to do with my attitude. Obviously, I can refer to the number of useful objects that I have (the number of chairs, desks, cars, etc.) without depending on a measure of the intensity of my desire for them. I could also refer to the amount of use I get from these objects (meaning the frequency with which I put them to use), and not the pleasure I derive from doing so.

I may also derive pleasure (or satisfaction) from the things I use, and I may do so to different degrees. An object may provide pleasure, but the measurement of its use does not depend on the degree of satisfaction it provides.

When modern economics refers to utility, it considers not the usefulness of the object but the subjective attitude of its owner or prospective owners. The notion of use is largely irrelevant to an economist who thinks this way. To such an economist, important conclusions depend on the notion of subjective desire, but not on those of usefulness or utility. Thus, the idea of consumer demand depends heavily on a notion of the subjective attitude of the consumer to the object he desires; it does not depend at all on the objective utility of the object.

A question remains, however, concerning the significance, of the concept of usefulness and utility in economics. If we were to introduce the objective notion of utility in place of the subjective ideas of desire and satisfaction, would this lead to a significantly different and more powerful understanding of economic affairs? When we introduced the concept of need, one of our primary claims was that need incorporates a force of necessity absent in the ideas of choice and preference. The work we do and relations we enter into to satisfy needs differ significantly from those motivated by preference. Our use of the term need leads us to explore an appropriate notion of utility. In the following, we build our interpretation of the economy on the ideas of need and objective utility, rather than preference and intensity of satisfaction. By so doing, we hope to demonstrate the objective quality of the fundamental relations of market economy, and to isolate the force of necessity that determines their structure and form of development.

Most useful objects are formed of matter—wool, metal, plastic, etc.—and are objects in a physical sense: they exist outside of us, and oppose us physically. Our immediate experience of them suggests that this makes them objective to us. The chair on which I sit keeps my body suspended so many inches above the floor, which keeps me suspended so many inches above the ground. Consider the following two ways of describing the chair:

Description 1: The object that suspends me above the ground has four small rubber cylinders, two-inches wide by three-fourths of an inch across. These cylinders are attached to the ends of two metal crossbars that meet at a point at which each is bisected. At this point, a metal cylinder extends upward for eight and one-half inches and screws into another metal crossbar, which suspends a metal square consisting of four pieces, each of which is seventeen inches long and three-fourths of an inch wide and attached at 90 degree angles. This square supports a piece of foam rubber enclosed by a piece of blue fabric. Two eleven-inch metal bars rise upward from the base of the fabric on each of two opposing sides.

A sixteen-inch-long piece of wood is attached to the top of each pair of bars. Attached to the pieces of wood is a second, somewhat smaller piece of rubber enclosed by fabric.

Description 2: I am sitting on a blue fabric and metal swivel chair on wheels.

We can make Description 1 much more detailed and precise by specifying the kind of fabric, the chemical composition of the metal, the ways in which the pieces are attached, etc. But by doing so, do we develop a more detailed and precise description of the chair considered as a useful object?

To answer this question, consider Description 2. Description 2 provides a concise yet adequate description of an object according to its use rather than its physical structure. In the case of a chair, the use directly incorporates certain physical relations (e.g., that it suspends my body above the ground), but to add a specification of those relations to the word chair would be redundant. Description 1 provides a poor and inadequate description of the chair as a useful object because it is virtually impossible to deduce the chair's utility from the description. Description 2 provides a very poor description of a physical object, since you cannot deduce physical construction from the word chair.

We can draw the following conclusion from our discussion of the chair: the word chair does not connote any determinate physical reality; nothing in the word connotes physical properties of an object. Yet the term chair does connote a reality that is objective for us.

While the word chair does not connote a specific material thing, it does specify a use. Whatever the material composition and physical structure of a chair, it must be something we sit on individually. A chair elevates us off the ground, and it separates us from others. When an object provides these services, it does the work of a chair. Description 1 detailed qualities the object had regardless of its relation to an individual and to his needs. The object of Description 1 was passive so far as the individual contemplating it was concerned. Description 2 of an object detailed qualities that it had exclusively in relation to the needs of the individual. This object only exists in relation (either potential or actual) to the needy individual who can make use of it. Without this relation, the physical object of Description 1 continues to exist, but the chair of Description 2 does not.

The work that an object does to satisfy needs is its use. To emphasize the social nature of consumption, we will use the term social practice to connote the things we do with an object in accordance with its use.[1] Thus, the word chair refers us to a particular social practice: a socially recognized mode of satisfying a socially recognized need.

Chairs fit into ways of life involving specific kinds of interpersonal relations. A society whose members sit cross-legged directly on the ground differs from one whose members sit at a table, each in his own chair, each elevated an equal distance above the ground. The chair establishes a social relation; it participates in a social practice. If I sit in a chair while you sit on the ground, our relation is marked by our differing degrees of elevation, both physical and social.

The social practice we identify with the chair is so complex that different kinds of chairs establish different social relations. A chair can be stern and unyielding or it can be soft and flexible, just as the social practice can have these qualities. A chair can be rich, expensive, even magnificent; or, it can be poor, cheap, and inconsequential. Place two individuals in these two types of chairs and you have two types of individuals, one rich, expensive, and magnificent, the other poor, cheap, and inconsequential. You are what you sit on.

Sitting on a chair, then, is a way of relating to others and a chair is an object that can only exist where the relevant way of relating exists. Man has no innate or natural need to "sit" above the ground suspended by an object that supports not only his bulk, but also, and more importantly, his separation from others while he interacts with them. This work of suspension and separation only needs to be done for the individual engaging in a specific social practice.

Using the chair requires participation in a social practice. This makes the chair a social object for its consumer. In using the chair to satisfy his individual need, and by using it in conformity with the appropriate social practice, the individual participates in an objective social reality. Only by so doing can the individual assure the social recognition of his needs and his individuality. Just as my needs are made socially objective by their recognition, the things that satisfy my needs are the social objects defined within social practices.

A useful object has a force of its own capable of directing the social practice in which its consumer participates. This makes the relationship between the good and the needy individual more complex than that suggested by the idea of subjective preference. The needy individual who owns the good has the right to establish his mastery over it by consuming it. Even while consumption of the good establishes its subordination to its owner's need, the social properties that make the object useful also dictate to its owner the form and manner of its consumption. Consumption simultaneously expresses the mastery of individual over object and the dependence of the individual on the object. The individual establishes the social character of his needs, and therefore of his person, by using goods in accordance with their social determination.

While needy individual and useful object both contribute to their relation—consumption—they contribute in different ways. In particular, when we say that the individual consumes the object while the object takes on the role of being consumed, this is no mere matter of terminology. The good has a complex social nature independent of its consumer that makes it an object for him. But the good has no will of its own. It exerts its power over the consumer in his act of consuming it not by subordinating the consumer to its own subjective ends (since it has none), but precisely by being subordinated to the consumer's need. The consumer uses the object to satisfy his needs. The good is the object, or means; the consumer is the subject who asserts the ends.

The consumption relation involves two further aspects: (1) Only when I use the object can it realize its destiny. I bring it to life; without my activity its utility is no more than a potential. (2) I use the object in a particular way that both conforms to its utility and satisfies my particular purpose. This means that I incorporate it into my mode of consumption. By so doing, I do not violate its objective utility, but make that utility contribute to a complex mode of life that gives that utility a specific meaning. This involves incorporating the particular good into a mode of consumption utilizing many goods simultaneously, and in a well-ordered and purposive manner.

A table may be used for writing a novel or for ordering the business affairs of an office. The table's use depends on who uses it; the consumer determines the use of the object by giving it a purpose within a mode of life. This fact does not conflict with the objective utility of the table. I do not make the object on which I write my novel a table by writing my novel on it. Regardless of what I do with it, so long as I respect its integrity as a table, it remains a table. I can write on it or I can organize my life on it and it remains a table. If I chop it up and use it to fuel my fire, it ceases to be a table.

What we have said thus far concerning use treats as given the social practice within which the good takes on meaning. For the individual this will normally be the case. If, however, we assume that this is always the case, we cannot account for change in use. Indeed, one way in which individuals assert their autonomy is by developing idiosyncratic practices that alter slightly or even profoundly a given social practice. The possibility of contributing to a change in use extends the meaning of the idea that in use a person asserts his will over an object.

We can introduce change without undermining our notion of objective use if we assume that innovation takes place within a well-defined context of meaning. When a person asserts his autonomy by redefining a social practice (or by defining a new one), his motivation remains to assert or express a socially meaningful sense of self. This means that while the innovation may surprise or shock others, it can still be made intelligible to them. We cannot treat Andy Warhol's use of a Campbell's soup can as though it directly participates in the social practice given expression, for example, by traditional use or by the advertising campaign developed by the Campbell's Soup Company. Nonetheless, Warhol employs the prevailing practice as his starting point. He intends to convey meaning to others (or more generally to participate in a dialogue) and indeed, his new use takes its meaning from the way it both continues and alters existing practice. The new use does not stand on its own.

For an innovation to have meaning, it must be intelligible; for the new use to be intelligible, it must depend on and be implicit in the old use. This requires that the new use constitute a determinate change from the old. Innovation does not violate the idea of objective use but extends it in an important direction. It turns out that this extension plays a central role in the development of the market (see Chapter 4).

PROPERTY

When I use a table as a part of my life, its use can take on a special association with my person: my purposes, my needs, my sense of self. I subordinate the table to me. I do so most decisively by making it my property. Since my general disposition over the object is the essence of the matter, the idea of property cannot govern (as the idea of utility can) its specific use. In this sense, property right has a formal character. My ownership of something does not require me to do anything in particular with it. I may consume it in various ways, or I may do nothing more than contemplate the fact that I own it. Acceptance of the idea that what I do with it is up to me makes it my property. Property right differs from need since need involves a specification of use while property right does not.[2] Put differently, when I think of the various things that I own as my property, I think of something they all have in common despite their different uses.

I can express this common feature of my property by setting a value on it. Each different object then becomes so much of my property, the only difference being the amount of property each represents. Thus, when I insure my belongings, I treat each particular piece of property as a sum of money. When I make a claim on my policy, I replace my property with money. When I do so, I do not change the amount of property I own, although its composition with respect to use may change. In this sense, the idea of property involves an abstraction from my particular needs and from my unique way of using the objects that satisfy my needs.

Does this abstraction make need and property right independent? The question is of vital importance. A fundamental premise of a private enterprise economy holds that property rights are independent of need, which excludes any idea of a right to income or wealth.

Important conclusions follow from this premise. On one side, my right to property does not depend on and therefore cannot be limited by my need for it. As a result, I may own property for which I have no need. I may own it exclusively for the purpose of ownership itself, and not because of an intention to consume it. This conclusion links a particular idea of property to the idea of the accumulation of wealth. On the other side, if I need something but do not own it, I have no right to it, and my need goes unsatisfied.

When we make property right and need independent, we provide a logical support for inequality not only in the distribution of wealth but also in the degree of need satisfaction. On one side we allow accumulation of wealth beyond need, and on the other property insufficient to satisfy need. The separation of property right from need justifies inequality even if it does not create it.

If we take an existing distribution of property as given then we restrict ourselves to concern for protection of property. Respect for property rights stems from respect for the integrity of the individual. But if we consider a system in flux, so that the amount, composition, and distribution of wealth are not already given, then we no longer need restrict our attention to respect for existing rights. Since property and property rights are coming into existence, we can also consider the origin of property and its ownership, or how claims arise to new property.

Thus, at a given point in time, I own a specific collection of objects (my house, my car, my clothes, etc.). My primary concern with regard to these objects considered as property is respect for my

ownership right regardless of how I choose to consume them.[3]   But
in considering the acquisition of more property, the recognition of
property rights may or may not suffice.

We will consider two ways of thinking about how property
comes into existence: (1) Appropriation by production—I claim a
right over a newly produced object because I caused it to be
produced. (2) Appropriation through use—I claim a right over an
object when I integrate that object into my mode of consumption.

One of the founders of the production-based approach was
John Locke, who linked property to labor and argued that the
individual has a right to the product of his labor.[4] For Locke, this
right followed from the premise that the individual as sole
"proprietor" of his person also owned his bodily functions including
those that make up the activity of laboring. Since the individual
owned his labor, he owned the product of his labor. The product,
in a sense, "embodied" the laboring of its producer, so that he who
owned the labor ipso facto owned the product.

This labor theory of property suggested limits to appropriation
and to the distribution of wealth. Appropriation has its first limit in
the laboring capacity of the individual. The labor theory of property
presumes that the laborer produces the product by himself and by
employing only implements that he also produced. Only when the
individual is the source of the product does it become exclusively
his property.

The labor theory of property severely limits individual claims
over property, since it restricts property to that produced by the
individual himself.[5] The labor theory also incorporates a latent
limitation of property by need. The individual employs his labor in
producing objects that become his property. The only reasonable
motivation for doing so would be the ability of those objects either
to satisfy his needs or to be used as means for purchasing objects
that satisfy those needs. The scale of production allowed for by the
labor theory of property depends on the individual's productive
capacity. This leaves little scope for the development of wealth. As a
result, both needs and the means to fulfill them remain at a
primitive level.

Classical political economy resolved this dilemma. While
retaining the idea that property originates in labor, it allowed the
individual to claim as his property the products of the labor of other
individuals.[6] This result was accomplished without violating the
spirit of the labor theory of property by introducing property in
labor. The labor market, in which labor time is exchanged for
wages, severed the laborer from ownership of his product. Thus

labor continued to produce property, but its amount was no longer limited by the laboring capacity of the individual.

The individual who hires laborers owns the product of their labor. This changes the idea of appropriation in a significant way. According to the original labor theory of property, I own something when I have produced it. According to the modified version of classical political economy, I own something when my property (including property in the labor of others) has produced it, i.e., when I have caused it to be produced. The first conception focuses on the direct producer (the laborer); the second directs our attention to the entrepreneur or capitalist. The capitalist owns the "means of production." In the simplest case, he purchases the labor time that produces the products. Because he owns the means of production, he owns its product. His means of production are the only real limit to his property.

If I own means of production that produce commodities whose sale yields a profit, then I own both my original property (my capital), and the profit it produces. Utilization of my property for the purpose of making property expands my property. Recognition of my right over means of production extends directly to recognition of my right over new property it produces. Thus, the formal idea of the recognition of property rights solves the problem of the distribution of new property; and it solves it by precluding need from bestowing a right to property. The distribution of newly produced wealth depends exclusively on the distribution of previously existing wealth. If previously existing wealth was originally newly produced wealth, then its distribution depends on the distribution that precedes it. The cycle can be continued backward indefinitely, and at each point the ownership of property will fully determine the distribution of the new wealth that it produces.

The logic of the labor theory of property, once modified in the classical direction to allow for a labor market, made existing property rights the origin of rights to newly produced property. The same logic can, however, be modified in a different direction to yield a radically different result.

In its original form, the labor theory asserted that a property right followed from a special relationship between producer and product. Because the laborer gave form to the object, and because that form accorded with the laborer's subjective qualities and purposes, the product bore a unique relation to the person who produced it. It was the property of the producer because it bore his personal mark.

If we think of an artist or craftsman, this idea begins to make sense. Artistic production creates an object that expresses the unique qualities of personality of the artist. A painting or sculpture (unlike a shirt, car, or frozen dinner) irrevocably and eternally remains identified with the individual who produced it. If we are familiar with an artist's work, we only need to look at (or, in the case of music, listen to) a new work to identify its author. According to the labor theory of property, this unique relationship between producer and product constitutes the basis of property right.

To the extent that property was produced predominantly by artists or artisans, the labor theory had a certain force. But when most property originates in a process with little or no dependence on the craftsmanship and artistry of the laborer, the theory loses its power. Today, the vast bulk of property bears no discernible connection to the personality of its producer. If property rights originate in the development of a unique relation between an individual and an object, labor can no longer be the origin of property.

Indeed, if we accept the idea that right derives from an investment of personality in an object, then production no longer qualifies as the basis of property right. This leaves us with two options. Either we continue to make production the source of rights to new property, in which case property right will not presume an investment of personality in the object; or we insist that property right implies an investment of personality in an object, in which case production cannot be the source of property right.

The second option emphasizes the way in which the individual attaches objects to his person. The property relation identifies the object with the individual personality so that the experience others have of the object implicates the owner (as when we experience a work of art; the artist is always implicated; we know who he is; and we learn something more about him). We have already identified such a relationship: consumption or use. Integration of an object into our mode of consumption identifies that object with our personality. It simultaneously gives a particular meaning to the object and a social manifestation to the personality of its consumer.

If we require the individual to make something his property by integrating it into his mode of life, then clearly property rights are limited by need. I cannot integrate an object into my mode of life unless the sustenance of that mode of life requires that object. And this implies that I can appropriate only things that I need.

This does not yet imply that I have a right to the things I need, but only that I must need something if I am to claim it as my property. The formal recognition of property right still holds force. This means that need and right are not synonymous. However much

I may need something, if someone else owns it, I have no right to it.

We can combine the formal notion of property right with a substantive notion of how something becomes the property of a particular person. If consumption enters into the activity of making something property, it follows that need will enter into the determination of the distribution of property; and it can do so without subverting the regime of private property (e.g., by equating need with right).

This last condition is very important, since in its absence the freedom of the individual would deteriorate. My freedom presumes my ability to articulate and satisfy a structure of need that is uniquely my own. I do this by consuming a specific set of goods. When I consume these goods, I give them a particular meaning relating to my mode of life. I must, therefore, dictate the particular manner of consumption of the object. I can do so because the object is recognized to be my property. Others recognize it as subject to my will and outside the limits of theirs. For me to fulfill my needs and realize the destiny of the object, I must be recognized as its owner. No one else can claim to determine how an object I own will be consumed by asserting their needs against mine.

Thus, ownership allows me to realize myself through my mode of consumption, and this result presupposes a fundamental distinction between need and right. But, as we have seen, it does not directly presuppose that need has nothing to do with the distribution of property.

Normally, ownership precedes consumption. But this does not mean that prospective consumption cannot provide a basis for property right. I may claim an object no one else owns because I need it. If this claim is recognized, then I own it before I use it, but the prospect of its use gives me the right of ownership.

We can arrive at this conclusion only in so far as goods come into existence in such a way as to leave open the question of ownership. If new property is the result of the use of existing property, then need cannot enter into determining its distribution. But if new property does not come into existence when existing property is put to use, need can enter into determining its distribution.

In order to resolve the issue, we must consider the question of private ownership over the means of production. As we will see later, when the means of production are privately owned, need and right are independent. But if they are not privately owned, space exists for interdependence between appropriation and need.

WEALTH

When my needs are those associated with asserting my individuality within society, the objects that satisfy my needs must also be my property. This requirements stems from what it means to use an object within a mode of life. When I use something, I treat it as an object, and I can only use things that I can properly treat as objects. When I treat something as an object, I subordinate it to my will; that is, I assert the ends that my use of the object will achieve. In this relation, I treat the object as, and fully make it, my property.

A market economy is a system of property relations. Its purpose includes providing the property required to satisfy individual needs. In addition to considering the origin and nature of property, economics must also consider the ability of the economy to provide the amount and kind of property adequate to satisfy those needs.

In considering the amount of property, economists have traditionally pursued two distinct lines of argument: (1) We can ground our analysis in the idea that the amount of property available limits the satisfaction of needs. If needs are insatiable and/or the amount of property is fixed independently of need, then needs can never be fully satisfied. This is the standpoint of scarcity, and of modern neoclassical economics, which treats property as a scarce resource. If we follow this line of argument, we will tend to think of an economy as a mechanism for the allocation of scarce resources among competing ends. (2) We can ground our analysis in the idea that individual needs limit or determine the amount of property the economy provides. As needs expand, the scale of social production of useful property will also grow. This is the standpoint of wealth, and of economics as the science of wealth. It was first established by Adam Smith, when he argued that the division of labor (the production of wealth) was limited by the extent of the market (the development of needs). When we have property adequate to satisfy our needs, we have wealth. The purpose of a modern economy (and especially of its growth and development) is to provide us with wealth.

Wealth, riches, luxury, abundance—these terms all connote the availability of the means to satisfy our needs. However, simply having the means to satisfy our needs does not make us wealthy. If we have only the barest subsistence needs, we are not poor since we do not feel a lack, but neither are we wealthy.[7] If we have the manifold needs of people in what Adam Smith refers to as "civilized society," and those needs are not satisfied, then we are poor. Wealth refers to the means for satisfying needs. But it also implies abundance, since having wealth means that we will be able to satisfy our needs. Thus, the term wealth connotes the means to satisfy needs in a very strong sense. The needs we have in civilized society differ from our needs in a natural state; they involve us in a social condition. Wealth satisfies a multiplicity of needs that change and develop with the growth and development of our personalities.

When we adopt the standpoint of scarcity, the amount of available "resources" becomes decisive because it defines the limits of need satisfaction. The idea of subjective desire can provide a foundation for the standpoint of scarcity, since it quantifies need and thus implicitly suggests a measurement of need against the means for its satisfaction. If desires are insatiable, then scarcity is inevitable.

When we adopt the standpoint of wealth, the amount of wealth in relation to needs becomes less important. The idea of social need provides support for this standpoint since it focuses attention on a qualitatively defined structure of need rather than a quantitatively defined degree of need satisfaction. As a result, the question of whether or not needs are satisfied takes precedence over the question of the degree to which they are satisfied.

Whether we adopt the standpoint of wealth or of scarcity depends on two considerations: (1) Our understanding of the determinants of the productive power of society (its capacity to produce wealth); and (2) our conception of the limits of social need.

Clearly, if the available means for satisfying need are fixed, then scarcity is likely to characterize the relation of need to the means for its satisfaction. The idea of "resources" captures this fixity. If wealth is ultimately composed of resources, then the amount of wealth has a fixed upper bound. Society may be able to change the "form" the resources take and adapt them more directly to the work of need satisfaction, but those resources have a fixed capacity to meet the needs of their owners. If wealth is limited by fixed resources, society may be unable to produce wealth according to the need of its members.

By contrast, if the amount of wealth depends on social production, society has the power to determine whether or not individual needs will be met. In this case, when needs remain unsatisfied, the economic institutions bear responsibility for failing to produce wealth adequate in quantity and form to satisfy those needs.

These alternatives involve dramatically different judgments concerning how wealth is produced and what limits its production. In Chapter 3, we consider this issue in detail since its resolution has a profound effect on our understanding of the potential for constituting a wealthy or civilized society.

The possibility of a wealthy society, however, depends as much on the condition of finite needs as it does on the possibility of producing wealth sufficient to satisfy those needs. If needs are unlimited, real wealth can never be achieved. In this case, the wealthier society seems to become, the more consumption engenders new and expanding needs, the more society falls short of satisfying needs, and the poorer members of society become. Illimitability of need implies a paradox: Needs once liberated from the limits of subsistence call forth a vast development of wealth that makes subsistence appear as a state of deprivation to individuals in society, while, in fact, it is only within society that an individual feels deprived. Real deprivation has its roots in the expansion and multiplication of need. Lacking the funds to finance a vacation in Europe, I feel deprived, even impoverished, by the parochialism that results from my lack of a European experience. The existence of wealth makes me poor when it stimulates in me a set of needs that I cannot fulfill.

In this respect, the distribution of property also plays a part in the debate between the two standpoints of wealth and scarcity. A sharply unequal distribution can create scarcity by stimulating the need of those at both ends of the scale. Poverty, then, is not simply the absence of wealth; it is the absence of wealth in the presence of wealth.

Does this mean that our needs in society are, in fact, illimitable? Put differently, can the individual always find a use for the things he does not have?

Let us focus on this last formulation of the question. For the individual to find a use for something, he must place it within his mode of consumption. If my sense of self emphasizes the exercise of intellect and culture to the exclusion of physical exertion, I will have no use for a pair of skis or a tennis racket. My needs are defined in accordance with a sedentary and cerebral mode of life. Similarly, if I think of myself as a practical sort of person, I will have no use for a Maserati. Thus, insofar as I have a clearly defined mode of life, it must exclude a wide range of needs associated with other modes of life. Indeed, this result follows directly from the link between consumption and individuality. My needs must be different from those of others; thus my needs cannot include all of theirs. The notion of social need implies that needs are self-limiting; i.e., they are limited by the structure they jointly define.

This result need not conflict with the change, development, and expansion of needs. With the development of my mode of life, new needs emerge so that my needs may not be fully satisfied at each point in time. Satisfaction of social need makes up the process of life in society. Only with the end of life does the process end. In this respect, we never completely satisfy our social needs.

The satisfaction of need can recreate that same need or create new needs. When I use my car, my need for a car expands and develops. When I have used up my car, I need a new car. This means that we do succeed in satisfying our needs without thereby arriving at a state of satiation or needlessness. When I have my car, I have no need for another car; my need for a car is satisfied. When I eat dinner, I do not need more food; my hunger has been satisfied. And yet, each act gives notice of a future need that I will have to find the means to satisfy. So long as we think in terms of social need and not subjective desire, this result holds. Because social needs are discrete and qualitative, they can be satisfied in principle. Because we can satisfy our needs, wealth and civilized life are goals we can sensibly pursue.

This result holds so long as our purpose in acquiring property remains its use to satisfy our particular needs. We do not allow for any other possibility when we root property in use. But if we retreat to the formal standpoint from which property rights involve no expectations regarding use, then my purpose in acquiring property need not be consumption in accordance with its utility. In this case, I can acquire property simply for the purpose of owning it.

This would not be irrational if the amount of property I own makes up an important element of my self-conception. When being wealthy becomes an end in itself, independent of any structure of need, the finiteness of need breaks down. If the idea of acquiring wealth in order to be as wealthy as possible becomes an element of my personality structure, then my need for wealth can never be satisfied since it does not fix upon a discrete group of useful objects.

Since this need for wealth can only be satisfied by degree—when we need goods for their contribution to our overall wealthiness—we can only satisfy our need to a degree. This undermines our conclusion that needs are discrete and can be satisfied. When I satisfy my need for a car by owning and using a Ford, my need for enhanced social position may remain unsatisfied. The link between need satisfaction and position in a social hierarchy makes need quantitative rather than qualitative and encourages us to shift the focus of our thinking from need (discrete) to desire (continuous).

The possibility that the pursuit of wealth as an end in itself will become an element of the individual's personality structure plays a prominent role in economic theory. Throughout the remaining chapters of this book, we will consider various aspects of this idea. We will see that the issue of a just distribution of wealth depends on whether we encourage the pursuit of wealth for its own sake to enter into personality structure.

To summarize our two alternatives: (1) We may think of needs as finite and discrete. This does not imply that the work of need fulfillment comes to an end; but it does imply that needs can be satisfied. (2) We may think of need as illimitable. When the work of becoming wealthy is made an end in itself, then the amount of wealth that we need has no limit. This is so because our object in acquiring wealth is not to satisfy particular needs but to be wealthy. This alternative cannot be reconciled with any argument that limits property right on the basis of need.

Our choice between these two alternatives bears on the possibility of identifying a just distribution of wealth in the following way. If use does not limit need, then we cannot have a right to the things we need. Clearly, if needs are illimitable, we can never acquire all the things we need; we can hardly have a right to a condition that we can never attain. By contrast, when needs are finite and property right presupposes use, basic elements for an argument concerning just distribution have been put in place. Thus, the issues of wealth versus scarcity and just distribution are closely bound together.

The link between the pursuit of status in a social hierarchy and need introduces a purpose into need satisfaction that goes beyond that considered up to this point. When we separate out this purpose, we find that it has broad implications. These implications concern the relationship between wealth and power, and therefore the relationship between economics and politics.

The term power refers to those attributes of persons that enable them to accomplish their ends as persons.[8] Power need not involve force. If in order to accomplish our ends we require the cooperation of others, we have power if we have the ability to gain their cooperation. Partly for this reason, wealth confers power and can be pursued in order to acquire the power it confers. An unequal distribution of wealth, by placing wealthy persons in a position to contribute to the satisfaction of the needs of the less wealthy, places those with wealth or with more wealth in a position to acquire the cooperation of those without wealth or with less wealth.

Power over others can also become an end in itself. In that case, power is the ability of the person to achieve his ends and the end itself. Just like wealth, power is now part of the person's sense of self, a component of his personality structure. When wealth and power become ends in themselves, they work together to define our position in a hierarchy of persons. Both contribute to establishing how much of a person we are, one by directly measuring the magnitude of our person in the magnitude of the wealth we own, the other by directly establishing the superiority of our ends over those of others (i.e., our power to make others work to achieve our ends).

When politics involves the pursuit of private ends, wealth and power become preeminent political currency. Wealth confers power and power can be used to acquire wealth. The ends of political and economic life become confused. They merge in the private interests of particular people. When we identify politics with the pursuit of private ends, then the distinction between politics and economics becomes a distinction between means to the same end. When society encourages the pursuit of position in a hierarchy of persons, both the economy and the state become means to the self-aggrandizement of persons.

MONEY

When needs involve the expression of individuality, change and development in needs and the means for satisfying them become an important part of social life. This means that the idea of change is an important part of a person's sense of his place in the world. Persons take responsibility for bringing about change (the needs are their own). To do so they must experience the potential for change as an attribute of the existing structure of need. The potential for change must be a part of daily life.

Consider the experience of hunger. If society identifies the means for satisfying hunger with some fixed substance, then this tends to exclude change in the manner of need satisfaction. If the word we use for the means to satisfy hunger specifies a particular object (wheat, rice, or the flesh of a specific animal), then we cannot so much as form the idea of change. If, however, we employ a word that connotes the means to satisfy hunger in general (e.g., "food"), then we can at least form such an idea. If I experience change in my needs, this encourages me to form the idea of new needs and of new means for their satisfaction. But for my needs to change, I must have already formed the idea that they are not fixed, and this idea must be part of daily life.

So far as particular classes of need are concerned, we have a set of words that capture this idea by defining need in abstraction from particular objects: food, housing, transportation, entertainment, clothing, etc. Each of these terms refers to a wide and changing variety of particular goods. We also have a term, wealth, that allows us to think of the means to satisfy needs without even the specification implied in terms like food and clothing. The idea of wealth involves an abstraction from particular sets of goods, so that wealth differs from any particular good, or any particular set of goods.

In this sense, we use the term wealth to achieve an abstraction. But when we make this abstraction, we in effect create a new reality irreducible to any set of particular useful objects. Indeed, this abstraction has a power of its own. When we form the idea of wealth, we give ourselves the power to form the idea of change and development of needs, and to act on that idea to bring about change and development.

When we form the idea of wealth, we participate in the work of creating a new reality, a reality different from the particular means for satisfying needs. Of course, for each of us who live in a society based on production of wealth, this new reality comes ready-made, so to speak. We do not make a decision to create the idea of wealth. Nonetheless, the idea of wealth motivates our activities in society and results from our collective commitment to ways of life involving wealth. In society, the idea gives birth to ways of life dependent on it, and those ways of life make the idea a social reality by incorporating it into everyday life. We assure that wealth will continue to exist by organizing our lives around the premise that wealth already does exist.

When we use the term wealth, we discover that our new reality has the properties of an object or thing. We own wealth; we pursue wealth; we produce wealth; we consume wealth. Our work of abstraction has created a new social object. This new social object, which captures the ability of wealth to exist independently of any particular set of useful objects, is what we think of as money.

We use money in two related ways: as a unit of measurement and as a social object. Both of these uses contribute to establishing wealth in abstraction from particular needs and objects.

When we measure particular goods, we use their natural units. These units do not allow us to sum different goods, such as cars and houses, since the units are inseparable from particular uses. We must then define units of wealth different from those of goods that compose it or to which it provides access. We already implied as much when we emphasized the importance of freeing or abstracting wealth from particular goods.

In the first instance, we use the term money to refer to the units—dollars, marks, pounds—that society uses to measure wealth once wealth has been distinguished from collections of useful objects. When you ask about the magnitude of someone's wealth, you do not expect to be answered with an inventory of his property, but with a number indicating the amount of wealth he has.

Of course, in any society that links wealth to status and in which status requires a certain mode of consumption, the ability to satisfy certain needs (and their manner of satisfaction) implies wealth. Ownership of a certain kind of house or car, a yacht or a private jet, may connote wealth. But it does so only because of the amount of money those objects represent. In our calculation, the particular pieces of property stand only as so many dollars. Where matters of wealth are concerned, monetary value always has pride of place.

Money is much more, however, than a mere unit of measurement. So long as we use money merely as a unit of measurement, wealth still consists of particular goods. But for the idea of wealth to have a real power in society, it must exist separate from particular goods; it must, that is, stand apart as a distinct social object. When money exists as an object, the idea of wealth as the general or abstract potential for satisfying need also exists as a tangible reality.

The money we carry in our pockets is no mere unit of account. It is also a social object that participates in a unique social practice. It is not only a unit for measuring wealth, but also a veritable piece of wealth, a bit of the stuff of which wealth is truly made. It must be so, since its units are the units of wealth and it is nothing more or less than so many of those units.

We can do two things with money that we cannot do without it. We can measure wealth without recourse to the units we use to measure goods, and we can hold our wealth in the form of an object that has no particular use.

Our ability to use money as a unit of measurement allows us to think about the particular goods we own as so much of our wealth; that is, we can measure those goods in "wealth units." This work of valuing our property draws a link between the particular good and the wealth of its owner; it allows the good to be a part of wealth. Once we have wealth units, we can think about wealth as made up of many particular useful objects, and we can think of those objects as pieces of wealth, retaining the idea that wealth does not satisfy any particular needs. When I say that I own a car worth $5,000, I assert both that I have the ability to satisfy a particular need (e.g., for transportation) in a particular way—I own a car—and also that I have a certain amount of wealth. I have placed a value on the car, and I have used money units to measure that value. Thus, my car not only satisfies a particular need, it can also be used to acquire the means (value) for satisfying need without prior specification.

In practice, the two uses of money get separated in the following way: We focus the term money on the object that is wealth without being any particular good—the piece of wealth as such. We use the term value to refer to the wealth units present in a useful object. We connect the two uses by using money as the wealth unit. A piece of money is a piece of wealth; it is value. A particular good has a value. The money unit is the unit of value.

CAPITAL 3

What makes society wealthy? An individual is wealthy when he has the means to satisfy his needs. Society is wealthy when it provides the means to satisfy the needs of its members, i.e., when its individual members are wealthy. But for society to be wealthy, an endowment of wealth adequate to satisfy the needs of individuals is not sufficient. According to François Quesnay, the founder of the Physiocratic school, true wealth must be renascent wealth. This means that a wealthy society has the capacity continually to renew and increase its wealth. A wealthy society knows how to produce wealth, a poor society does not.

The term produce connotes the process of transforming inputs into outputs viewed on the basis of the result. Whenever we can isolate a result, we can work our way back to a process that produced it. Viewed from the standpoint of production, the product determines the process. When we produce a good, we organize production so as to assure that its result has the useful properties intended. We translate our objective, useful property into a process. We can produce wealth when both inputs and process are appropriate to that end.

Any transformation can be thought of as production if we isolate a result in this way. We can, for example, think of an apple tree producing apples. The tree absorbs certain inputs—nutrients from the soil, water, sunlight—and uses those inputs to produce apples. It transforms them into apples. To assure this outcome, the inputs must be appropriate: the proper amount of sunlight and rainfall, the correct mixture of nutrients in the soil. Apple trees only grow and produce apples where the combination of inputs works out. The transformation process must also be appropriate. A plum tree will not produce apples since it will process, or work up, the inputs in a different way. Production of apples involves a process of transformation that incorporates information (in this case biochemical information) specifying the internal process to its result.

In order for us to think of the life-cycle of an apple tree as a production process, we must isolate the apple and consider it in a special sense a result. Nothing in the tree's life-cycle, however, directly supports this way of thinking. If the seed in the apple successfully takes root, it becomes the starting point rather than the end point of a process that we can think of as the production of the apple tree. The life-cycle of the tree forms a connected process. This process has no result other than its own continuation. When we leave the apple tree and the apple alone, we lose the idea of a result or a product; and when we lose the ability to isolate a result, we also lose the idea of a production process.

Nothing in the life-cycle of an apple tree suggests either the idea of production or of a product. However, if we harvest the apples and consume them, we impose an end (to which the apple tree is, of course, indifferent) that allows us to think of apples as products. Similarly, if we harvest the apple tree, we can think of it as a product. The idea of production then implies the assertion of a human purpose: the use of something to satisfy human needs. In nature processes are ongoing; they do not define results, and they do not produce anything. However, even when we do nothing more than contemplate nature, we begin to separate product from process. We do so because we do not perceive nature as a whole, but only that part we find relevant. Once we isolate an element of a natural process, we begin the work of distinguishing product from process.

We can, of course, go well beyond contemplating nature by imposing our ends. We do this when we make use of natural products, such as a tree to build a house.

The formation of a product does not occur by accident. On the contrary, the process is organized to assure that, under normal operation, it produces the expected result. As we have seen, this specification of process to result implies that the result exists latently within the process. Information concerning the product must be present to organize and direct the process.

Thus, for example, if I want to construct a birdhouse out of wood, I must have the necessary inputs: wood, screws, drill, paint, etc. In addition, I must have information about the product adequate to direct me in my work. In this case, I must have a detailed plan involving a sequence of operations determined by the intended shape of the final result.

This specification of the process to its product plays a crucial role in our investigation of wealth. Production may involve transformation of inputs into outputs, but for the output to be wealth, the inputs and process must contain information concerning the specific and distinctive qualities of wealth. Nothing can come out of a process that does not enter it either directly as an input, or indirectly as an organizing principle directing the work of transforming inputs into the intended product. Apple trees cannot be made to produce carrots because they do not "know" how to produce carrots.

The questions that arise for us then are: What kinds of inputs and what mode of processing inputs will produce wealth? What does society need in order to produce wealth?

LAND, LABOR, AND CAPITAL

Different economic theories provide different answers to these questions. These answers specify a source of wealth. Three sources have attracted special attention: land, labor, and accumulated wealth (capital).

Most production processes employ in some sense all three types of inputs. Such processes occur in space using some material inputs and in this sense depend on land. They also employ both labor and produced inputs. To this extent, we could claim that the three inputs jointly make up the source of wealth. Indeed, the traditional neoclassical theory depends heavily on the assumption that land, labor, and capital can each be thought of as a "factor of production" in a process that bestows no special status on any one of the three. No particular factor has a special role to play; on the contrary, the factors are all "substitutable" one for the other.

Such an approach contrasts sharply with classical economics, which emphasizes the unique role played by one or the other of the three inputs. The classical approach begins to make sense when we look more closely at production. When we do so, we find ourselves forced, as the classical economists were, to isolate one factor in accounting for the outcome of the process (i.e., the form and the amount of wealth produced).

In the earliest classical theories, land was the dominant factor. While the idea that wealth originates in the land infects all classical thinking to one degree or another, only François Quesnay and the

Physiocratic school adopt the principle that land alone is the source of all wealth.

The idea that land produces wealth means that (1) the amount of wealth depends on the fertility of the land considered as an innate natural quality (what David Ricardo refers to as the "original and indestructible powers of the soil"), and (2) the utilities of the individual "pieces" of wealth derive from their natural attributes. If a product (e.g., corn) provides nutrition, then this means that nature provides a substance capable of contributing to the individual's biological sustenance.

In this case, production does not take place on the land (as when a factory occupies a certain location), but in the land (as when plants grow rooted in the soil). The foundation of a building roots it in the earth, but only in a passive sense. The building does not grow out of the earth, nor does it take sustenance from the earth. If we want to think of the land as the real origin of wealth, then we must restrict wealth to those things nature provides and that are directly or indirectly nurtured by the earth: things that grow on trees, sprout from the ground, roam the plains, or even, by extension, swim in the seas.

If we think in this way about growing corn, for example, we consider it a process that man and his implements may assist, but one that ultimately goes on outside of man's control. We cannot, as yet, build a machine that produces corn in the way we produce shoes or lawnmowers. We may at best modify the natural phases of the growth process. The rhythms of the process are biological rhythms. The sequence of events that turn the seed into the adult plant establishes a unified natural process.

Obviously, in this case land (or nature) is not a mere factor among others. It is the real source of the product. And if the product is wealth, land is the source of wealth. Indeed, when certain of the classical economists employed the idea of a "stuff of life," they did so partly in order to make land the source of wealth. When wealth consists of this stuff, land creates it.

But this result follows only if wealth consists of things existing in nature. In our treatment of the stuff of life, we found that attempting to do so caused severe problems. Obviously, dependence on nature to form the objects that satisfy our needs limits, even eliminates, the role of human purposes. Objects that satisfy social needs do not grow on trees, sprout from the ground, or roam the plains. Nature provides means for its own survival; man in society must provide for his.

The classical economists recognized this point. Having asserted that all wealth comes from the land, the classical theorist goes on to note that the land, by itself, produces no wealth, but only the barest subsistence.[1] Individuals made to subsist on the land become as much natural objects as the stuff of life that provides their means of subsistence. When nature determines the form and magnitude of the product, that product will only sustain us in our "savage state"; it will not provide us with the wealth required to satisfy our civilized needs.

At this point, the classical economists put labor to work on the land in order to make the land produce wealth. But when we put labor to work on the land, do we make the land produce wealth, or do we merely provide labor with a place in which it can produce wealth?

Having brought labor to work on the land, and thereby given up the idea that production of wealth was a purely natural process, the next step was for economists to find in labor what had been lost in the land: the unifying force in the process of the production of wealth. We have already considered the idea that property originates in labor. When a craftsman shapes a product, the land recedes into the background. The craftsman occupies space and may employ materials originating in nature, but he does not allow nature to form the product. Now, instead, the laborer forms a product according to an idea embodying a human purpose. Natural processes and natural products play a passive role, while the mental and physical capacities of the worker dictate the shape of the product and the amount produced.

We can always think of labor and nature cooperating in production. But we still need to specify which of the two actually forms the product, and because it gives shape to the product, also determines the phases, rhythm, and productivity of its production process. If the process produces wealth, or a component of wealth, the factor that plays this part will be the origin of wealth.

We have already identified difficulties that arise when we try to think of land as the factor that makes wealth. As we saw in Chapter 2, however, similar difficulties arise when we try to find ways of making labor produce wealth. We first introduced labor in order to make the land produce wealth. But when the laborer has only the land to work with, there is very little he can do beyond appropriating natural products: hunting, fishing, gathering. Labor cannot make the land produce anything different from what the land produces by itself. No amount of work will make an automobile sprout from the ground or a pair of shoes grow on a tree. For labor to provide us with something other than natural products, labor must have something other than land to work with.

A natural starting point for thinking about this "something" other than land is the implements or tools the worker employs. These implements allow the worker to do what the land did previously: determine the shape of the product. But in this case, the process of shaping a product realizes an idea that the worker has, so that the molding process involves subjective ends rather than biological imperatives. The laborer dominates the process. He makes his implements work for him and subordinates them to his purposes. If the implements are relatively simple tools, they depend on the worker to give them purpose.

When the laborer dominates the process, the process gives him an opportunity to express unique features of his personality. The shape of the product accords with purposes linked to the individual producer, so that qualities of the product depend on his subjective characteristics (in Adam Smith's words, his "skill, dexterity, and judgment").

The product no longer provides simply for the natural subsistence of the species. Does it, however, contribute to the wealth required to satisfy social needs? To some extent, no doubt, we must answer this question affirmatively. Prior to the development of capitalistic economic organization, access to the products of skilled craftsmen was a mark of wealth (as of course was ownership of land). Even today, ownership of, for example, an original painting embodying the personality of the artist indicates wealth. Thus, the growth of craftsmanship involves the growth of wealth.

Consumption subordinates wealth to the needs of its owner rather than those of its producer. This encourages the producer to consider the product in relation to the personality of prospective consumers rather than to his own. Production for the market has this quality. When we think of a firm producing cars, we think of it attempting to design a car that will appeal not primarily to the chairman of its board of directors or to the engineer who works out the details of the design, but to the prospective consumer. What imposes this orientation on labor and focuses that labor on the end of producing wealth?

Adam Smith answers this question by introducing the division of labor. Division of labor connotes a rearrangement of the work process so as to allocate individual elements to individual workers. The resulting specialization of labor creates narrowly defined and routinized tasks that reduce the amount of labor time required to produce the product.

In the most famous example from *The Wealth of Nations,* Smith describes how the process for producing pins could be divided into a sequence of distinct activities: cutting the wire, sharpening one end, blunting the other end, etc. By specializing among these tasks, workers can produce many more pins in a given time period. This increase in productivity marks the orientation of a process toward producing wealth.

What does society need in order to make wealth? Neither land nor labor, answers Smith, but division of labor. The division of labor has, however, certain preconditions and implications that Smith does not ignore.

When classical economics introduces the division of labor, the idea of a craftsman gives way to that of a laborer in the modern sense who becomes, in the extreme case best described by Karl Marx, an appendage of a machine. Subjective qualities of individual workers cease to be relevant. Each worker now represents simply so much labor time. The worker no longer impresses his personality on the product. He no longer oversees the process as a whole, nor does he provide its unifying force.

The nature and the unity of the process is dictated by the shape of the product. But the shape of the product is no longer an idea that the laborer has prior to and during the process, and that he imposes on the materials. Each worker now engages in a routine and mechanical function. No single worker can provide unity for the whole process. We must find another factor capable of organizing and directing labor toward the production of wealth. This organization of the production process around a single purpose, which originally was the work of nature and was given over to labor, now passes to capital.

If we hold to the classical idea of division of labor, we can think of this organizing force as a kind of labor: the labor of managing or directing a group of laborers. It seems natural to think of the agency responsible for assuring that the individual workers labor toward a common end as a kind of laborer: someone who tells each worker what to do in accordance with an overall plan. The organization of the plan depends, of course, on the technical specifications of the product. We still have a labor process; only, in this case, the unifying agent is a superlaborer.

What our director/manager or superlaborer does differs dramatically, however, from the work of the skilled craftsman. Recall that for the craftsman, skill, dexterity, and judgment remain crucial. The craftsman can impress aspects of his particular personality on the product, while the director of a group of laborers cannot.

The director cannot treat the labor he oversees as part of his own labor. He cannot make his laborers express his personality through their labor. He can, however, treat them each as abstract or general labor time divorced equally from his personality and from their own. When he does this, he considers the labor requirements of production in a purely mechanical way. Moreover, his own "superlabor" also takes on a mechanical quality.

The purpose of production precedes the act. Before we begin production, we must have an idea of the good and its associated social practice. Production imposes this idea on the individual elements (including the individual workers) that make up the production process. But this idea is not the private purpose of an individual (worker or manager); it is the idea of a good with a social meaning. As such, it can be put to use by many individuals with distinct private ends. Prior to being used this way, however, the object has no connection with any person. Thus, while the idea must be imposed on the process as its organizing principle, this imposition need not be the work of some particular individual.

When the leader of an orchestra conducts a symphony, he organizes the contributions of each individual musician under a unified purpose. He also imposes a subjective end (his idea so to speak) on the members of the orchestra. This subjective end combines purposes built into the musical score by its composer with those contributed by the conductor. When the work is played under the direction of a particular conductor, it bears his mark.

Now, imagine the same symphony conducted electronically. When the score calls for particular instruments to play particular passages, a light goes on to signal the appropriate musicians. If the composer writes the score so as to make possible the mechanization of all the relevant signals (not just the particular notes, but how they are to be played, including the precise decibel level and exact duration), he makes the conductor superfluous. The subjective intent the composer built into the score has now been built into a machine that directs electronically the realization of that end through the employment of the skills of particular musicians. Since the music does not depend on a conductor, the composer can be assured that the piece will sound the same each time it is played. No doubt it will sound more than a little mechanical, and perhaps like something less than music. If we think of the spirit of the performance as an important component of music, our result is very poor music, or not music at all. It may be that, in the case of music, we are better off with no performance than with one lacking spirit.

But what if our purpose is not the performance of a musical

score, but the production of a toaster? We can think of the idea of the toaster as a score that organizes the contributions of different laborers. And we can think of the score impressing itself on the laborers mechanically. Consider an assembly line. The assembly line resembles our mechanized score since it informs each laborer when to begin his contribution and how long his contribution should last. When we mechanized the performance of our piece of music in this way, the result was a spiritless, and inferior, form of music. Is the spirit of the toaster similarly diminished when we dispense with our director/manager?

Since, in the case of the toaster, the product need bear no qualities traceable to a director, the answer must be no. Unlike a symphony, the production process of a toaster best realizes its purpose when it follows the prior specifications of its original designers (the engineers who "composed" the idea of the toaster and designed a process for realizing that idea). When we buy a toaster, we are uninterested in the personality of its designer; we neither know nor care to know the identities of the designers and engineers involved. We are only concerned with how we can use the product, and this means that our concern is not with the personality of its producer, but with our own personality.

When we hear George Solti conduct the Chicago Symphony Orchestra, what we hear is his rendition of a piece of music; something we can never make wholly, or essentially, our own. We do not use it, though we may enjoy it, appreciate it, and even learn from it. When we buy a toaster, we expect neither to appreciate nor to learn from it, but only to use it. By the nature of useful goods, we lose nothing and gain much when we dispense with the director/manager. We gain separability of the product from the personality of its producer and this allows us better to use it in accordance with the dictates of our own.

We can take this result one step further. What if we not only replaced the conductor of the symphony with an electronic device, but also replaced each member of the orchestra with a device capable of producing the range of sounds their instruments produced? The original score would be translated into a series of signals transmitted by the electronic conductor to the various devices capable of producing the required sounds. The result? Music without musicians. By doing this, we hardly breathe spirit into the performance, and the outcome will no doubt be an even less ideal musical performance than when we only gave up the conductor. The more we mechanize the "production process," the more we lose qualities we associate with the idea of music.

But in the case of our toaster, nothing is lost by this and everything is gained, and for the same reasons as before. The work of producing the toaster can be done by machines controlled by other machines. The toaster hardly suffers from this sort of upbringing. On the contrary, it positively thrives on it. A production process organized in this way would realize, in extreme form, the idea of a capitalistic process.

Capital has replaced labor as the factor that organizes production. The idea of the product now is built into the mechanism that produces it. Not land, not labor, but capital provides the source of wealth. Even if a certain amount of labor remains, the idea of the product does not reside in the mind of the workers, but in the machinery with which they work. The machinery molds the materials in accordance with an idea incorporated into its structure. The mechanism directs and unifies the phases and rhythms of the process. The worker contributes his labor time, but plays an otherwise passive role.

Since the machinery embodies the idea of a particular good (its product), the machinery must be designed and produced with that idea in mind. Nature can no more produce a machine than it can produce the machine's product. Machines make up an important part of society's accumulated wealth. This accumulated wealth, or capital, rests on land, and employs labor, but subordinates each to its particular purpose. While the three "factors" work together, one always dominates, setting the pace, organizing the process, and embodying the end. The other factors play a passive role.

The shape of the product depends fundamentally on which factor dominates the process. When land dominates, the product has a natural shape that accords with its part in the natural cycle. If such a product satisfies a human need other than by accident, it does so because the human need remains more natural than human, and because species imperatives still dominate over social needs.

When labor dominates, human purpose plays a primary role. The laborer consciously asserts this purpose. Even when he does nothing more than cook his food, he proclaims the inadequacy of natural products to his ends, which are no longer dominated by species imperatives. Since the laborer forms the product according to his subjective purpose, he impresses his personality on the product.

When capital dominates, it organizes the process so that the product becomes associated with particular individuals and with the dictates of their personalities. Social needs have priority over species imperatives. But unlike the product of the labor process, the good produced by capital does not bear the mark of its producer's personality. When capital produces a useful object, its producer has no personality to impose on the product. This quality makes the product well suited to take on an association with the personality of its consumer.

In modern society, we find examples of all three kinds of production processes (especially of the last two). For our purposes, however, discovering examples of the three cases is less important than understanding distinctions between land, labor, and capital-based production processes. The terms land, labor, and capital connote three different and alternative ways of organizing production. The significance of this result has to do with our understanding of the origins of wealth. Of the three production processes, capital has a special association with wealth.

Capital is wealth devoted to making wealth, especially (though not exclusively) its production. The amount of wealth produced depends on the amount of capital available and the knowledge built into it. This does not imply that the amount of wealth available to society has no limit, only that the supply of factors other than capital (e.g., land and labor) does not ultimately limit the amount of wealth. Instead, the amount of wealth available depends on the way in which society has made use of its wealth in the past and on the technical know-how built into its capital stock.

The idea that capital produces wealth undermines the standpoint of scarcity discussed in Chapter 2. When the amount of wealth depends on the past use of wealth to build a capital stock, there is a sense in which the wealth of society depends on its past devotion to the work of making itself wealthy. The more society devotes itself to this task, and the better it understands the source of wealth in capital accumulation, the more likely it is to succeed in providing the wealth it needs. The better society understands where wealth comes from, and the more society can produce wealth according to need, the less a fixed endowment of wealth determines the degree of need satisfaction.

We pointed out in Chapter 2 that if we think the amount of wealth is fixed by the availability of scarce resources, then need satisfaction will be limited by resource endowment. In this case, it will be difficult to argue that individuals have a right to the things they need since that would imply a right to property that does not exist. The standpoint of wealth, which gains support from the idea that capital produces wealth, allows for the possibility of a right to satisfy needs since it allows need to play a part in determining the amount of wealth available. This is especially the case insofar as needs help determine the pace and direction of capital accumulation.

THE FIRM

If by capital we mean an organizing principle that animates a production process, then we have more in mind than a mere technical apparatus—we have in mind a producing organization. This organization corresponds to what we call a firm. The purpose that the firm hopes to achieve by producing something useful is not the satisfaction of its own private or individual need. Since the organization is not a person, it has no needs associated with the realization of, or expression of, its personality. Indeed, the firm does not consume its products at all, but hopes to sell them in the market. Yet the firm must have some objective of its own when it produces goods for others. What is this objective?

If we recall our original definition of capital, an answer to this question begins to emerge. We originally defined capital as wealth devoted to making wealth. Generally, to produce wealth we must produce something useful, but utility does not measure the degree to which something useful contributes to wealth. Instead, we count the wealth units present in our product when we attempt to measure the wealth that we have produced. So far as the product has value (that is, can be measured in wealth units), we can think of that value as the objective of its producer.

When production takes place within a firm, production and consumption are separated not only in time and place, but also by their proximate objectives. An economy that organizes production capitalistically defines an objective for the producer distinct from that of consumption. But at the same time, this objective must have the power to direct the firm to produce those things that satisfy consumer needs. The ability of a market economy to accomplish this is among its most remarkable features.

The solution to the problem is found in the conditions necessary for a coherent and consistent measurement of goods in value. These conditions relate to the pricing of commodities and to the specification of an objective and a consistent value unit (money). We have already identified the first requirement of valuation: the abstraction of the idea of wealth from its identification with particular useful products.

With money units for measurement, the idea that wealth can be acquired without accumulating particular useful objects makes sense. The abstraction we associate with the idea of money makes possible a reorientation of production from the immediate satisfaction of particular need. Thus, "making money" can become the subjective purpose animating a social organization, in this case the firm. When we have the idea of wealth, we can also have the idea of making wealth. Indeed, the first idea gives birth to the second.

Whether making money can be the subjective purpose of an individual oriented toward realizing and expressing his personality is a question that we will consider in Chapter 5. Obviously, the idea that becoming wealthy can be the motivating purpose of an individual's mode of life originates in the abstraction of wealth from its direct association with particular goods and particular needs. The traditional idea of the capitalist describes an individual who devotes his life to, and defines his personality on the basis of, the process of making wealth and becoming wealthy. While historically some in society have oriented themselves to acquiring wealth as an end in itself, it does not follow that they thereby succeeded in realizing an individual sense of self. Indeed, an important question arises regarding the extent to which the capitalist's mode of life satisfies the requirements of individual self-expression and self-realization. This question has to do, however, less with capital than with its ownership. Regardless of who owns capital, its objective must be to make wealth. The issues surrounding the ability of the capitalist's mode of life to sustain his individuality are related to the issues surrounding the private ownership of capital. We will return to these matters in Chapter 5.

We can think of the firm as a social organization oriented to making wealth. When we say that firms strive to make wealth we do not, of course, mean that the firm actually produces money. It still produces particular useful things; but it thinks about those things as if they were units of money. How does the firm determine what goods to produce given that it has no need for its own product? By answering this question, we gain insight into the way the market reconciles the firm's orientation to making money with the necessity that it produce objects that satisfy individual needs.

The issue can be put somewhat differently: When the firm makes wealth, it uses wealth as its means of production. In this sense, the firm consumes (or uses up) the wealth it employs. When the means of production have been consumed, they have given up their value. Capitalist production uses wealth to produce wealth, and this implies that wealth is consumed in the production of wealth. Since some wealth is produced and some is consumed, whether I have made wealth or not depends on the proportions.

The true amount of wealth produced is the difference between the value of the wealth consumed and the value of its product. In economics, this difference is termed the net product, or profit. Consumption of wealth only produces wealth when the net product is greater than zero. We can now define the objective of the firm more precisely as the production of profit.

The firm produces goods but only as a by-product of the production of profit. All goods that have value are potential sources of profit for the firm. In order to produce profit, the firm does not have to produce any particular object. Firms can produce different products at different times, and they can produce more than one product at any given time. In this sense, the firm's objective is a general one, and we can think of the firm as a generalized producing unit.

Firms determine what goods to produce on the basis of the profit they expect the production of that good to yield. Does this in any way assure that the firm will produce something that individuals need? Can profit be that objective distinct from the satisfaction of need that, nonetheless, has the power to direct firms to produce useful objects capable of satisfying needs? For this to be the case, profit must be sensitive to needs. In particular, (1) only products that satisfy need can yield profit, and (2) when the things individuals need are not being adequately produced, profit must provide the information and motivation necessary to assure that firms take steps to rectify the problem. Economic analysis is concerned with the complex relationship between individual need and profitability. This relationship must assure that the ends of the producer and the ends of the consumer work together.

The economy's ability to support a consistent calculation of profitability assures two important results: (1) It assures the separability of producer from consumer necessary to the production of wealth. Insofar as profitability is sensitive to the needs of consumers, it also provides the link that unites production with consumption. (2) Profit provides the firm with a generalized objective. Firms can produce different products and still attain the same objective. This means that the goods produced by firms can change and so adapt to changing needs. The specific goods that make up society's wealth can change within the limits of profit-making by firms. Were firms committed to producing particular goods rather than profit, this adaptation would not be possible.

Those conditions allowing a rational calculation of profitability provide an environment for the production of wealth and the satisfaction of individual need. The organization of the market affects price determination and capital accumulation. It ultimately determines whether a calculation of profitability can be made. Since the market is a system of exchange transactions, we now turn to an investigation of the exchange relationship.

THE MARKET 4

INTERPERSONAL EXCHANGE

If we need only those things that nature provides us directly (e.g., things that grow on trees or roam the plains), and if we do not need very many of them, then we might each produce the things that we consume (or, at least, we might produce them in small groups). But if we need articles of wealth, we will not be able to produce all, or even very many, of the things we need. If I have the skill to build a house, I probably cannot produce a car, or a radio, or even the things I need for dinner. Even if I know how to build a house, I probably do not know how to make the things I would use to build the house (bricks, glass, nails, etc.). In a wealthy society, individuals must go about the work of acquiring most of the things they need from others. What kinds of relations do we enter into when we acquire the things which satisfy our social needs?

Economics has an answer to this question that focuses attention on individual freedom. Economists argue that exchange is the way individuals acquire the things they need from others without giving up their freedom. Two different lines of argument support this conclusion.

First, we can think of exchange as a voluntary transaction that allows for the exercise of choice and therefore supports individual freedom and individual welfare. This argument connects freedom to the market on the basis of the idea of choice. Second, we can think of exchange as a relation between property owners requiring the recognition of property rights. Since exchange confirms individual rights, it supports individual freedom. While these two lines of

73

argument seem closely connected, they are by no means equivalent. When we respect property rights, we allow the property owner to determine how to employ his property. Respect for property right can imply that the individual determines the composition of his consumption basket. As we pointed out in Chapter 1, however, this idea does not imply free choice if the individual has real needs. Thus, we can connect exchange to the notion of freedom through the idea of rights without assuming that the individual chooses in the strong sense. It turns out that different types of exchange correspond to different ways of linking freedom to markets (the choice-based approach and the rights-based approach). In this chapter, we consider these different types of exchange.

We begin with the idea that exchange relates particular individuals. We will call this interpersonal exchange. In *The Wealth of Nations,* Adam Smith provides us with an example of interpersonal exchange. Two individuals arise one morning to face a new day, and to consider different activities with which they might occupy themselves during the day. These individuals have no special talents or unique endowments. In fact, they so resemble each other in their capabilities that each faces the same alternatives. For simplicity, Smith assumes that only two alternatives exist: beaver hunting and deer hunting.

At the beginning of the day, neither individual has anything to exchange. Naturally, then, each immediately sets about the work of acquiring some property. One hunts beaver, the other deer. Having successfully completed his day's work, each returns with his means of exchange and sets about finding someone to bargain with.

At this point, Smith introduces a peculiar wrinkle. Since each individual could equally have done the work of the other, each knows the true value of the other's property: the amount of his own labor that he has saved when he acquires a commodity by exchange rather than work. Thus, if it takes two hours for me to capture a beaver and four hours to capture a deer, then one deer must be worth two beavers to me.

This argument should strike an odd note. If I want to consume deer meat, and at the outset of the day I have the option of hunting beaver or deer, why would I capture beaver in order to exchange for deer rather than simply hunting deer in the first place?

We might salvage the example in the following way. What if neither individual knows what he wants at the beginning of the day (or maybe they think they know, but get it wrong)? Perhaps the last thing you want to do at the end of a day spent hunting beaver is to eat one. Now we begin to see a basis for exchange. At the end of the day, each individual possesses something useful (a dead deer or beaver) that he does not want. Why not strike a bargain to get what you want in exchange for what you have?

This might happen, but if it did, it would no longer follow that the rate of exchange must depend on the relative amount of work devoted to acquiring the two dead animals. The sun is setting; the day is over. Each hunter has got what he's got, including the hunger built up during a day's hard work. The fact that in four hours spent the next day he could acquire what he wants now makes no difference both because he wants it now (he needs it for dinner), and because if he did spend four hours the next day acquiring what he wants today, there is no way of assuring that he will still want it when he's got it.

What determines the rate of exchange? Smith has an answer that fits better than labor time: "the higgling and bargaining of the market." What does this refer to? Two individuals meet, each owning something the other wants. Each agrees to recognize the property right of the other, so that to acquire what he wants each must convince the other to give up freely what he owns. The motive that the individual appeals to in order to achieve his private end—acquisition of the other's property—is the other's self-interest. Each achieves his private end by contributing to the achievement of the private end of another. I can motivate the owner of the deer meat to give me some of his property that I want by offering to give him some of my property, dead beaver, that he wants.

The rate of exchange depends on the amount of dead beaver required to motivate the deer hunter to part with his dead deer, and vice versa. Labor time has little to do with the outcome, which depends on the relative intensity of the property owners' desires for the two kinds of property. If the deer owner does not really mind eating dead deer, but would mildly prefer dead beaver, while the owner of the dead beavers has come to abhor the very sight of beaver dead or alive, we might expect the terms of exchange to favor deer over beaver; i.e., the deer price of beaver (the amount of deer required to purchase a unit of beaver) will be relatively low (beavers are cheap relative to deer).

The owner of the beaver will not, however, automatically offer his beaver at a low price. If he wants as much deer as he can get, he might offer his beavers at a high price. It then passes to the deer owner to refuse the deal and offer a lower price for beaver, i.e., offer his deer at a high price. The outcome depends on the fortitude of each participant in the bargaining process. Presumably, this is what Smith has in mind when he refers to the "higgling and bargaining of the market."

Smith introduces the labor time needed to acquire commodities in order to avoid the conclusion that price depends on bargaining power. The calculation of labor cost helps us determine the rate of exchange prior to the actual encounter between property owners in the market. Since I have produced the property that I bring to market, and I could have produced the property that you bring to market, I know the price at which the two properties "ought" to exchange before I ever get to the market.

The beaver and deer example may seem a little peculiar, but this result is not. I might take my money and use it to set myself up in business—say as a carpenter. I purchase equipment and materials and rent the necessary space. With my equipment and materials, I produce a desk. Because I have produced the desk, I can make a rough calculation of its cost: the value of the materials and the equipment used, together with the part of the rent that corresponds to the time I spent in the shop making the desk.

Since I have no use for the desk myself, my producing the desk only makes sense if I can sell it; and, given its cost, producing and selling the desk only makes sense if I can sell at a price that at least equals the cost. If I sell the desk above its cost, I might think of the margin as my income from producing the desk. I might still be prepared to bargain with a potential buyer over the price of the desk, but now I will only bargain over a range of price limited by the cost of the desk.

When I produced the desk, the range for bargaining over price narrowed. If I take my income to be a cost (for example, a wage for my labor), then that range disappears; I know what the price ought to be before I know who will buy the desk. This makes the price independent of the attributes of the persons who own the properties being exchanged, causing the exchange to lose its interpersonal quality.

Smith attempts to account for this aspect of price determination by introducing the concept of natural price. When commodities exchange at their natural prices, they yield revenues to their producers that cover the costs of production plus normal profit. The introduction of natural price indicates that the classical economists were well aware of the problem discussed here and made an effort to connect exchange to costs of production.[1]

Smith first argued that beaver and deer must exchange according to the amount of labor required to produce them in order to make the exchange rate independent of personality. But because he sets up the example as an example of interpersonal exchange, the labor condition tends to lose out and higgling and bargaining take over. Since interpersonal exchange depends on the relative desires and endowments of property owners, it inevitably leads more to a notion of bargaining and away from any notion of a "fair" price.

Costs of production define limits within which bargaining makes sense. These limits equal the allowable range of variation in the incomes of the two property owners. When you come into my shop to buy a desk, you offer me a specific amount of money in exchange. If this amount falls short of the cost of the desk, I will very likely turn you down. I might also make a counteroffer sufficient to cover costs and provide me with a net revenue adequate to satisfy my needs. You might then counter with another offer that is higher than your first but lower than mine. This price still covers my costs, but provides me with a smaller income so that fewer of my personal needs will be satisfied.

In this kind of market, my ability to satisfy my needs depends on finding someone whose needs will be satisfied by something I own (a desk). I may decide to have fewer needs satisfied, rather than none at all. I thus sell you the desk at a low price and eat fried chicken instead of poached salmon for dinner. Of course, if you do not happen to come into my shop, I might have no dinner at all. The market based on interpersonal exchange provides no assurance that needs will be satisfied, or that they will be satisfied in a given way.

Interpersonal exchange involves no overt coercion. Goods can be acquired only by free exchange. In this sense, interpersonal exchange supports individual freedom. Interpersonal exchange presumes the recognition of property rights but not their extension to the right of an individual to receive fair value for his property. Under interpersonal exchange, there is no such thing as a fair price. The absence of a notion of fair price allows individual incomes to vary with bargaining power. This means that individuals can use the market for self-aggrandizement at the expense of others. Thus, the reciprocity of a market rooted in interpersonal exchange is also a reciprocity of greed.

This kind of market appears differently depending on how we look at it. We could say that the market forces each individual, in the pursuit of his self-interest, to serve the interests of others. Or we could say that the market encourages, even forces, each individual, in the pursuit of his self-interest, to exploit the weaknesses of others and gain his end at their expense. Both arguments can be supported and, indeed, they make the same point in two different ways.

When we exchange property, we accept the idea of using each other as a means to our private ends. Because exchange is reciprocal, however, we do not thereby reduce another person to a mere instrument for us. We can work for others while retaining our independence.

When someone holds me up at gunpoint and takes my money, I experience a diminution of my wealth. If we ignore the possibility that I might be insured, robbery adversely affects my level of need satisfaction. But the trauma associated with being robbed does not end with my realization that I am now poorer. Regardless of the magnitude of my financial loss, my psychic response to my experience of the interpersonal relation "robbery" will differ from my response to the relation "exchange." Robbery violates my sense of myself as an autonomous person. Compared to the damage that my self-respect suffers, the loss of money seems relatively unimportant. Robbery denies me my property rights. Recognition of such rights precludes others from using me as a mere means to their ends.

Interpersonal exchange rests on a foundation of property rights. To this extent, such exchange sustains individual freedom. But the voluntary quality of this type of transaction also makes it dependent on different persons finding a coincidence of needs and properties. We can see this quality of interpersonal exchange most clearly in the case of barter (nonmonetary exchange). Each party to the exchange owns an object that the other party needs. Each acts directly as the means to the other's ends. Exchange takes place only when each party thinks that the exchange will make them better off. If each individual can satisfy his needs with things he already owns, but not as well, then his participation in the exchange is truly voluntary. He need not exchange; he does so only when he chooses to. Individuals make choices when they have the option of doing something different. If freedom means choice, the consistency of exchange with freedom depends on the individual's ability to get by (even if less well) without exchange.[2]

In the beaver and deer example, exchange will make the deer hunter better off since he prefers beaver; But if he prefers deer, he consumes what he has and no exchange takes place. For him, freedom means that he only gives up something he has in exchange for something he would rather have. Of course, if he cannot survive on what he owns, he exchanges not because he chooses to, but because he must.

When individuals can satisfy their needs with the things they own and exchange only because they can acquire things they prefer, then exchange allows "freedom of choice." When money intervenes, this result loses some of its force. Since I cannot satisfy my needs with money, I must use it to buy things I need. Even though I own the money and no individual can force me to give it up, I use it to buy things not by choice but by necessity.

We can draw a further conclusion from the study of interpersonal exchange. A market based on interpersonal exchange cannot support the idea that the individual has a right to satisfy his needs. Interpersonal exchange makes access to the things we need contingent on our endowments, and on relative prices. Obviously, for exchange to take place our initial endowments must lack some of the things we need. Furthermore, others must be endowed with the things we need. Whether we satisfy our needs will depend on prices, which are not determined to assure a predetermined degree of need satisfaction.

IMPERSONAL EXCHANGE

In the history of economic thought, interpersonal exchange is the form of exchange we encounter most frequently. Even modern treatments of the price system assume that transactions involve individuals (directly or indirectly) on both sides. Only on this basis can price determination depend exclusively on individual preference and endowment.

Oddly enough, we hardly ever encounter interpersonal exchange during the everyday business of need satisfaction. We rarely, if ever, acquire the things we need from other individuals who own them. To be sure, when I purchase a loaf of bread in a supermarket, I hand over my money to a person who gives me the bread in return. The person who sells me the bread does not, however, own it. In reality, I do not enter into an exchange with the person at the checkout counter. When we consider this case, we begin to move from interpersonal to impersonal exchange.

When we consider exchange an interpersonal relation, then each exchange must be treated individually as a unique event. This is because the attributes of the parties involved (i.e., their preferences and endowments) determine the parameters of the exchange. When we consider exchange between a needy individual and a capitalist firm, each individual exchange takes on a different significance. Since the firm concerns itself with profitmaking, it can treat each unit of output as if it were nothing more than potential revenue or profit. The firm treats each sale as the realization of that potential, which undermines the idea that each sale should be treated as a unique event. Instead, each sale represents so much more of the same thing to the firm.

Since the firm's goal is profitmaking, the contribution the sale of a single commodity makes to achieving that goal depends on its value. The product's utility has importance only as it bears on that value. It follows that the sale of the individual good contributes to, but does not fully accomplish, the firm's goal.

This result contrasts sharply with that of interpersonal exchange. Under interpersonal exchange, each party acquires something that satisfies their need. When I purchase the desk you have for sale, I acquire the means to satisfy my need for a writing surface. Two or three desks will satisfy my need no better than one. In this sense, I leave the exchange with my need satisfied, at least potentially.

Unlike the consumer, however, the firm leaves each exchange unsatisfied. No individual sale can directly or indirectly satisfy its need for profit. Each sale can contribute to that goal, but no sale, taken by itself, can achieve it. And unlike the individuals engaged in interpersonal exchange, the firm places each exchange within a larger context of exchanging. The individual sale makes up one component of the firm's market. It is only within the context of that market that the individual exchange takes on a meaning for the firm.

The consumer starts from his particular need. This gives the individual exchange meaning for him; it is the means by which he acquires a good capable of satisfying his need. For the firm, the starting point is the revenue, especially the net revenue, to be gained from the sale of many commodities. Thus, for the firm, the individual exchange gains its meaning from the mass of exchanges of which it forms a part.

For General Motors, the sale of one car gains its significance from its contribution to sales volume in a given period. If GM decides to produce a small, four-cylinder, fuel-efficient car, it does so not because it believes that there is one consumer who needs such a car, but because it believes that this car will satisfy a more general social need. If GM cannot sell a large number of these small cars, then it makes no sense for it to sell one car.

This example allows us to isolate the fundamental difference between interpersonal and impersonal (or capitalistic) exchange. Each interpersonal exchange must be considered a unique event governed in all its dimensions by the personalities involved. Each instance of capitalistic exchange must be considered one among a class of identical events that can be understood without reference to any particular individual.

We can make this point more concrete by contrasting the sales efforts under the two forms of exchange. The sales effort under interpersonal exchange involves a bargaining process between two individuals that leads directly to a particular exchange. The sales effort is linked to the actual exchange, and each exchange involves a separate sales effort. Under impersonal exchange, sales effort and exchange are separated. One sales effort supports a large group of individual sales.

In a sense, the ideal exchange precedes and establishes the basis for the actual exchange. The firm attempts to impress the consumer with the idea of its product. If this succeeds, the consumer will take the steps leading to a purchase.

When General Motors markets a new car, it does so not by seeking out particular consumers and trying to convince each individually to purchase a car. Instead, it orients an advertising campaign toward a specific class of consumers defined, for example, by age, income, and lifestyle. GM works to expose as large a proportion of this group as possible to the idea of a car tailored to their needs.

Advertising depicts an attractive ideal family with its new car: fuel efficient yet roomy, sensible yet luxurious. The consumer sees himself and his family becoming more like the ideal family when he buys the ideal family's car. The word precedes the deed; and off goes the consumer ready to purchase a piece of "The American Dream."

A unique event takes place under impersonal exchange. The consumer acquires a good he can use to express his personality. By consuming the good, the consumer solicits recognition for particular features of his self-conception. Yet the object used for this highly personal end was produced and marketed not for this particular consumer, but for a whole class of consumers. General Motors produces a car that an individual consumer finds uniquely appropriate to his sense of self and style of life; and General Motors does this without ever "knowing" that individual.

This implies nothing pernicious so long as needs are socially determined. Indeed, impersonal exchange facilitates the satisfaction of social needs in a uniquely appropriate way. Under impersonal exchange, the consumer acts as an independent agent who buys only those things he needs. Yet, while the consumer acts freely and under his own direction, he does not act alone. He acts in concert with a class of consumers, and under the guidance of the ideal consumer. The image in the advertisement binds together a group of consumers with a common purpose: construction of a lifestyle consistent with their individual self-conceptions.

This does not mean that the consumer will successfully realize the ideal. Purchase of what one manufacturer calls the "sensible luxury car" may or may not help the consumer make his family into the attractive ideal family. Nonetheless, the goal gives meaning to the purchase and subsequent consumption. In this respect, impersonal exchange has a meaning for the consumer different from that of interpersonal exchange.

Oddly, interpersonal exchange seems more of a social event because it counterposes two particular people in a face-to-face interaction. When we restrict ourselves to thinking of social relations as encounters between people, we tend to think of impersonal exchange as asocial. Whether it is depends on what we think makes something part of our social condition. Two alternatives bear consideration. One emphasizes the encounter between two persons whose particular purposes drive them into, or force them to create, a social event. The other emphasizes the prior construction of a social meaning not created by the individual. The social event (the purchase of a commodity) aids the individual in realizing a social ideal. The participants in interpersonal exchange construct their own social reality within, and for the duration of, the exchange; they do not participate in the predetermined reality of a socially constructed event. Under impersonal exchange, the individual participates in an established social practice.

When we make the face-to-face encounter the preeminent social event, we identify our social condition with particular social interactions. We tend to absorb any larger social reality into those particular relations. When we make the pursuit of a socially created idea a significant element of our social lives, we do not limit our social relations to those involving face-to-face interactions, nor do we assume that the meaning of social events can be equated with the clashing desires of persons meeting face-to-face. This way of thinking about our social condition leads us to emphasize impersonal exchange.

The prior construction of impersonal exchange as an ideal event also requires that the determination of price precede the transaction. Firms incur certain determinable costs in producing commodities. These costs logically precede the sale and place limits on the acceptable terms of exchange. The price that prevails in a particular exchange does not depend on the conditions of that exchange—that is, the particular personalities and endowments.

The classical economists used the term intrinsic value to describe this quality of exchange. When David Ricardo asserts that price is "intrinsic and not arbitrary," he has in mind the independence of price with respect to any unique or arbitrary characteristics of the exchangers. The price that prevails under impersonal exchange does not depend on who actually buys the commodity. Such a price does not discriminate among persons; it is a fair price in that it treats all persons alike.

Intrinsic, or objective, value plays a part in exchange only when two conditions have been met: (1) rational cost calculation based on the production of the commodity precedes the exchange, and (2) the terms of the particular exchange are determined by an ideal. When these conditions have been met, the seller can set the price (at least within narrow limits) prior to exchange. Price setting confirms the dependence of the particular exchange on a mutually understood ideal.

Price setting helps to make the exchange objective to the buyer. Before we buy a hat, we first confirm that the particular object under consideration *is* a hat. We inspect it, we try it on, we solicit assurances from a salesperson. We satisfy ourselves that the object in question conforms to an ideal. We then seek out the price tag in order to learn the price. The price tag provides us with some assurance that the price is "fair" in the above sense. We may find the sticker price exorbitant, but it is the price of the hat: not *my* price, or *your* price, but *the* price.

Impersonal exchange confirms individual property rights. No one can force you to use your money, or the property that you buy with it, in a way inconsistent with your own needs. You determine how to dispose of your money income. Since impersonal exchange excludes coercion by others, it supports individual freedom.

Firms produce and market commodities without a specific consumer in mind. In effect, they make a variety of commodities available to each consumer. Since firms make a variety of commodities available to the consumer without forcing him to consume any one, they provide the consumer with freedom of choice. From the standpoint of the firm, consumers choose among the firm's products, and among the products of various firms.

While the firm does not constrain the consumer, it does not follow that the consumer acts without constraint. For the consumer to satisfy his needs, he must purchase some of the products made available to him by firms. If those needs derive from a sense of self based on a socially constructed ideal, the individual must do what he can to satisfy them by purchasing the appropriate commodities. Firms provide individuals with freedom of choice, but individuals do not choose freely.

If my sense of self sends me in pursuit of a red sports car, then I will feel diminished if I cannot acquire such a car. Unable to satisfy my need, I feel a loss of identity and suffer psychic pain. If firms produce red sports cars, then they make the good capable of satisfying my need available to me. They leave the decision whether to buy it or not up to me. They do not know me and my needs. They have no right either to determine what I need or to make me purchase something I do not need. The firm respects my right to life, liberty, and especially the pursuit of happiness.

If by free choice we mean nothing more than the absence of another determining what I consume, then my purchase of a red sports car is a free choice. But if by free choice we mean an unconstrained, even undetermined, decision, then my purchase of the car has nothing to do with choice. Impersonal exchange can conform to the demands of individual freedom without assuming that individuals make choices.

Instead of using the idea of choice to capture the way impersonal exchange respects individual freedom, we could use the idea of rights. Firms recognize the individual's right to determine, on the basis of his own needs, what he will purchase. We can define freedom as a way of life within a regime based on respect for rights. If one of these rights is the right to own private property, then impersonal exchange can help to assure individual freedom. It can do so even where individuals base decisions on need. Indeed, because impersonal exchange incorporates a social construction of need (the relation of the consumer to the ideal), it is uniquely appropriate to the work of satisfying socially determined needs.

Within the sphere of economics, the term freedom can be used either to connote individual choice or respect for individual rights. Impersonal exchange provides respect for individual rights but does not depend on, and is in some ways inconsistent with, the idea of free choice.

DIRECT DISTRIBUTION

Whenever acquisition of the things we need requires exchange, our ability to satisfy our needs will depend on the means of exchange that we own and on the prices of commodities that we need. We can also read this proposition in reverse: when limits exist to society's ability to provide for the satisfaction of individual needs, society can impose these limits through the price mechanism.

Assume that we have a certain amount of money to distribute to individuals as their incomes. We can accomplish this distribution in various ways. We could give every individual the same amount of income. We could package differently sized bundles of income and distribute them at random so that individuals have different amounts of income, but not according to any rule. We could distribute income in proportion to height or weight. We could also make individuals work for their income, and pay them according to attributes of their work: its length, the amount of skill involved, the kind of talent required, the intensity of our desire for its unique products, etc. If we use this last option, we can even subsume income distribution under exchange by having individuals sell their working ability in a market in order to acquire income according to the price of that ability.

However we distribute money incomes, the individual's ability to satisfy his needs will depend on: (1) the rule used to distribute income, which determines the amount he gets; (2) the specific commodities he needs; and (3) the prices of these commodities.

Giving same-size bundles of income seems most equitable, but it may not be. If individuals have different needs whose satisfaction requires acquisition of different bundles of goods, and if these different bundles have different costs, equality of income distribution will lead to inequality of need satisfaction. Thus, even assuming equality a legitimate goal, it does not follow that distribution of same-size bundles of income to different people will help achieve that goal. Of course, it is not at all obvious that equality of need satisfaction ought to be our goal. Indeed, in a regime of individualized needs, equality of need satisfaction may not even be a meaningful idea, since individual needs can differ so widely.

If needs differ in this way, we can identify equality of need satisfaction only under certain limiting conditions. If individual needs are unlimited, everyone falls equally short of need satisfaction whatever their income. If individual needs are finite, and if we have sufficient wealth to satisfy those needs, we can provide for the full satisfaction of all needs. In this sense, we can provide an equal measure of satisfaction to everyone.

Impersonal exchange preserves the individual's freedom to determine how to satisfy his needs given his income and the prices of commodities. This works especially well when the relation of individual need to social wealth restricts need satisfaction in some way. When there is, so to speak, not enough wealth to go around, the market can allow individual self-expression in consumption within the constraints that social wealth places on need satisfaction.

When we have productive capacity adequate to satisfy needs, exchange might still prove useful insofar as the value calculations (e.g., of profitability) play an important part in conveying information regarding individual need (demand) to the units of production. When no needs are unsatisfied, however, another possibility exists: direct distribution. Consumers might simply appropriate the things they need without providing any quid pro quo.

This will not work when some needs must remain unsatisfied. In that case, decisions must be made regarding which needs the individual satisfies, and which he does not. If we give him money and send him into the market, then we allow him to decide which needs to satisfy. Exchange allows the individual to make that decision—direct distribution does not. In this respect, where some of the individual's needs must go unsatisfied, the market accords better with individual freedom than does direct distribution.

The problem that arises under direct distribution, even where we have the productive capacity to fully satisfy needs, concerns the producer's inability to anticipate the individual's needs so that he can devote himself to producing the appropriate goods. We can solve the problem of anticipation by assuming that needs never change. Individuals have different needs, but the needs associated with individual modes of life once set, remain forever fixed. Under these circumstances, past experience can fully guide the producer in determining what goods to produce. Furthermore, once producers determine which needs to satisfy, they only need to repeat periodically the production of the appropriate goods. Once production has taken place, the consumer claims the things he needs. Direct distribution allows the individual to govern his behavior according to the dictates of his own needs. Since firms produce those things they know consumers need, they have no interest in coercing consumers to acquire their products. Under these circumstances, direct distribution is consistent with individual freedom.

Under direct distribution, consumers have no incomes and goods have no prices. We employ direct distribution, for example, when individuals have a right to things they need. Society assures the exercise of this right by making the appropriate goods available and by making individual need a sufficient basis for the individual's claim to those goods.

Assume that I need a new car and, in particular, that my need can only be satisfied by a car exhibiting certain features: It must be a sports car because I think of myself as a sporty person; it must have a design that I find aesthetically pleasing and a color I find attractive; it must have upholstery in a color that subtly offsets the exterior paint; it must have an engine with certain technical features appropriate to the uses I have in mind, and so on. Assume, further, that I need this car because an identical car, which I had up until last Thursday, was demolished beyond repair when I just missed a curve while driving 87 miles per hour on a mountain road. Miraculously, I have survived the accident but am not the smallest bit wiser for the experience, so I want to replace the car as quickly as possible. Assume, finally, that the firm that produces this car has hired a statistician to calculate (1) the number of individuals sufficiently unbalanced to need a sports car capable of just missing a turn on a mountain road at 87 miles per hour; (2) the periodic rate at which these individuals can be expected to demolish their cars beyond repair; and (3) the probability that those individuals will survive the accident without suffering either an attack of good sense or sufficient bodily harm to keep them off the road. With this information, the firm will know how many new cars to produce each week. When the survivors of the latest accidents, older but no wiser, limp into the showroom, they will find a shiny new car waiting for each of them.

Direct distribution works well for all parties. I continue to find the good capable of satisfying my need available to me when I need it. The firm knows what to produce and when to produce it. Direct distribution works well because my need, however self-destructive, never changes.

The problem of anticipation has to do with changing needs. Direct distribution does not deal well with needs that change, nor does it work well with the process of forming new needs. Since producers do not sell products, they have no motivation to engage in a sales effort. Where, then, did I get the idea that high-speed mountain driving would set me free?

We may have chosen an odd example for direct distribution. My decision to buy a car involves my sense of self, and for that reason my motivation has to do with expressing my individuality. Since expressing individuality requires differentiation of persons, it also implies variety and variability of needs. This quality militates against the stability and predictability of needs required to make direct distribution work. Individual needs may not be the proper raw material for direct distribution.

The individual also has needs that do not involve the expression of his personality (at least, not in principle). Examples might include health care, education, garbage collection, and police services. The integrity of the individual may well depend on an adequate supply of these goods and services, but it does not require that they be tailored to his sense of self. To be sure, you may need to have a stolen car retrieved, while I need to have a broken leg set. In this sense, we use these services differently, depending on our circumstances. But my need to have my leg set and your need to have your car retrieved do not arise out of our efforts to establish our individual identities.

My sense of self will not diminish if the methods used to repair my leg do not differ from those used on everyone else. The doctor knows how to satisfy my need without knowing who I am. I have no reason for insisting that my leg be set in accordance with unique qualities of my personality. Because of this, I have no reason to insist on the market as the proper medium through which I acquire the service capable of satisfying my need. We might, then, agree that such services should be made available to all individuals equally, although they may be used differently.

When such goods and services play an essential part in preserving the integrity of the individual (his continuing as a person), we have a good argument for providing them on the basis of need and therefore by means of direct distribution.

Practical problems arise when we attempt to use direct distribution to satisfy inappropriate wants. Under circumstances of changing or insatiable need, the attempt to employ direct distribution introduces inequities. In a private enterprise system, inappropriate circumstances for direct distribution are ubiquitous. By connecting need satisfaction to the pursuit of wealth and to position in a hierarchy of wealth, private enterprise encourages a limitless expansion of needs. If, under these circumstances, we provide some particular good or service free of charge, demand will inevitably exceed supply and direct distribution will break down. When this happens, the resulting practical difficulties transform direct distribution into a competing method of allocation: rationing. The resulting allocation will appear arbitrary in relation both to market allocation and to the original intent of direct distribution. The point to emphasize is that the feasibility of direct distribution depends on social context and not on innate qualities of human nature, natural scarcity, or organizational constraints defined in the abstract.

It is not part of our purpose to address the concrete practical concerns of actual distribution processes, but only the contexts under which different methods of distribution have meaning. When a method of distribution makes no sense in a particular context, the practical issues are moot. When that method has a meaning in a well-defined context, we can address those practical concerns.

Interpersonal exchange presumes the recognition of property rights and the individual's freedom to pursue private interest through relations with others. Since we acquire the things we need from others, interpersonal exchange cannot recognize any right of the individual to the things he needs (other than his right to acquire them by exchange when their owners make them available). Whether the individual will satisfy his needs depends on his endowments and the prices of commodities. Prices depend on bargaining. Nothing assures that their levels will make the satisfaction of any particular individual's needs possible. Interpersonal exchange does not provide a framework within which needs can take on a social meaning. Each exchange creates its own interpersonal context; it does not form part of a social order.

Impersonal exchange also presumes the recognition of property rights, but it does not require that individuals seek out others to acquire the things they need. Since individuals continue to acquire goods through exchange, they have no right to satisfy their needs. The individual has the right to pursue need satisfaction in the market, but will normally fall short in his efforts. Given the prices of commodities, he will only satisfy those needs that his income allows him to satisfy.

Under impersonal exchange, individuals acquire the things they need not by providing others with the things they need, but by spending their money incomes on goods produced by firms. While impersonal exchange does not recognize a right of the individual to satisfy his needs, it may be consistent with the idea that individuals have the right to an income. We might think of this as a right to satisfy some part of individual needs. This part depends on the income provided to the individual, the prices of commodities, and the individual's own decisions concerning the disposal of his income.

Under impersonal exchange, each exchange takes place within a larger social context. The construction of the ideal act of consumption supports the social determination of needs. The individual treats the terms of exchange as objective facts.

Direct distribution can respect the property rights of individuals. When sufficient wealth exists to satisfy individual needs, that wealth may be distributed according to need. After its distribution, the wealth becomes the property of individuals. Direct distribution presupposes that individuals have a right to the things they need. It runs into difficulty, however, in dealing with the formation of needs and with a system of changing needs.

Direct distribution has been used to satisfy those needs independent of the expression of distinctive qualities of individual personalities. If we divide needs into those that differentiate between persons and those which do not, we can apply impersonal exchange and direct distribution to the respective sets of needs. Can we apply the idea of rights directly to the second group? In order to apply the idea of rights to this group of needs, we must allow the individual to determine when and how he will satisfy them. By assuring the provision of a good or service when needed, we do not necessarily recognize a right to that good or service. Whether our provision implies recognition of a right depends on who determines when and how the good or service will be provided.

Consider the example medical care. Do I have a right to open heart surgery? For such a right to exist, society must have an obligation to provide it to me simply because I think I need it or because I want it. But if society only has an obligation to provide me with surgery when a doctor judges that I need it, then access to surgery does not involve exercise of a right. Indeed, the absence of rights may facilitate acceptance of the social obligation by eliminating the connection between the need and individual self-expression. Our freedom and independence need not suffer when satisfaction of such needs takes place under the direction of others.

If we want to argue for a social obligation in medical care, we will have difficulty doing so using the idea of rights. On what basis, then, can we make such an argument? Logically, we could extend the claim that medical care, while needed, does not involve individual self-expression, to the conclusion that the market must therefore be inappropriate to its provision. Since markets have a special association with provision of those goods and services needed by the individual when he wants to express his individuality through consumption, the market serves no useful purpose in areas that do not involve individual self-expression.

Allowing individuals to determine how much health care or police protection they receive does not enhance their freedom. It only provides self-determination in areas that do not involve the individual's sense of self. The often heard claim that government provision of health care will lead to inefficiency and abuse by encouraging overuse of health care facilities totally ignores the way market provision of health care assures exactly those abuses. The market does this by allowing desire for health care plus ability to pay to establish a claim for care independent of need. The free market allows those who can afford it to acquire as much health care as they want rather than as much as they need.

We can void this conclusion by arguing that the need for health care involves individual self-expression in the same way as does the need for a particular kind of car or a particular color tie. This would immediately place all individual needs, whether social or psychological, on the same footing. When we do this, we deny the distinctiveness of individual needs (the need to be an individual in society), and the distinctive social purpose of markets in contributing to the provision of such needs.

We cannot apply the idea of rights to those needs that are independent of individual self-expression, although we can argue against their provision through the market. Can we argue that individuals have a right to those things that satisfy needs associated with expressing and realizing a sense of self? If I have a right to the things that satisfy my needs, then I must be able to acquire those things at will. Because of this, we can only apply the idea of rights directly if we have wealth sufficient to assure full satisfaction of all consumption needs. If we do not have sufficient wealth to satisfy all such needs, we might still entertain the idea of a right to income that recognizes individuals have a right to satisfy their needs, but do not have the right to satisfy any particular need. We have not yet presented a case for such rights, but we can begin to see how the analysis of need and right links up with the treatment of market organization.

PRICE DETERMINATION

The theory of price determination rests on a foundation created by the analysis of need and production. The classical theory of prices (the theory of natural price or price of production) accounts for rates of exchange in a world characterized by subsistence needs and what Piero Sraffa termed "production of commodities by means of commodities." Neoclassical theory attempts to determine relative prices on the basis of preference and scarce (nonreproducible) resources. Since our interpretation of need differs from both the classical and the neoclassical, we would expect a price theory based on it to have certain distinctive features.

In this and the following section, we indicate some of those distinctive features. To do so, we present the bare outline of a theory of prices and distribution. In order to makes this outline simple and brief, we focus directly on the part played by social need and abstract from other important aspects of price determination and economic growth. Thus we emphasize in particular the part played by consumer demand but give only brief attention to competition between firms within an industry. This can hardly be considered a rigorous account of price determination, and no such claim will be made. Our outline of the theory focuses on selected features and abstracts from others; it aims to direct attention to the way a change in the concept of need affects the more concrete concerns of economics (price determination and economic growth).

Under interpersonal exchange, we can say very little about price determination because the price will depend on circumstances associated with particular exchanges. The usual appeals to supply and demand, preference orderings, and factor scarcities may serve to systematize the little that we can say about these kinds of exchange, but the normal apparatus of price theory tells us little more than that prices depend on accidents of endowments and preferences. Under "perfect competition," as defined in textbooks, we can say something about the simultaneous determination of many prices, and of a single price applicable to a large number of exchanges. But having made the various assumptions demanded by perfect competition, we still learn little more than that prices depend on accidents of individual preference and endowment.

If we are to say something interesting about the determinants of exchange, we must turn to impersonal exchange. Under impersonal exchange, the problem of price determination becomes one of finding a price that simultaneously yields profit to the firm and makes the commodity accessible to the consumer.

Assume that the firm has produced a product that individuals need, and has made this fact known to them. Only one condition remains to be satisfied for the sale to take place. Consumers must be able to buy the commodity, given its price and their incomes. For a coincidence of purpose between producer and consumer to develop into an exchange, the relationship of price to income must be such as to make the sale of the commodity feasible. In this section, we take a closer look at the determinants of price in relation to consumer income. We will take price to be a variable for the firm, and consider how consumer income places a limit on price setting under different assumptions about the distribution of income.[3]

Assume that each consumer begins with a set amount of money income. The consumer is to use this income to acquire the set of goods that will allow him to experience a mode of life expressive of his sense of self. We will not consider how this mode of life comes into existence, but only how it governs the individual's consumption decisions once the individual has committed himself to it. Since the mode of life already exists for the individual, he uses his current income to maintain it and further its development.

In order to preserve his identity, the consumer must reproduce his way of life by replacing used up means of consumption. This replacement consumption must be financed out of current income. Consider the use of income to acquire food. If an individual has a sense of self involving an active orientation toward maintaining a healthy body, his diet will consist predominantly of fresh fruits and vegetables, fish and chicken, whole wheat bread, etc. Each week these foods must be replaced and for this purpose, the individual must set aside part of his income. The amount may not be rigidly fixed, but it will mainly fluctuate within fairly narrow limits. The individual budgets a certain amount for food each month based on the kinds of foods he eats and their prices. If the individual ate mainly red meat, pasta, and Wonder Bread, he would need to set aside a different amount of money income in order to maintain his lifestyle during what might be his abbreviated lifespan. Given the requirements for reproducing a mode of life, the consumer must set aside a certain amount of income to be used in acquiring the necessary commodities. We will call this committed income, since the continuation of an existing style of life commits the consumer to spending part of his income on replacements for goods used up. The amount of his committed income depends on the consumer's mode of life and on the prices of commodities.

This suggests one further point. Consumers can only develop commitments to styles of life they can afford. Living within your income means developing a mode of life appropriate to that income. Experience of a mode of consumption over an extended period confirms the associated sense of personal identity. This will tend to confirm the specific needs that must be satisfied on a periodic basis. If the individual successfully identifies himself with a mode of consumption made available to him by his income, his income will be adequate to satisfy his needs.

Any change in our consumption pattern will require giving up elements currently included, and replacing them with new ones. Such substitution can occur, but if we restrict change in modes of consumption to substitution, we exclude an important dimension of individual modes of life. How does an individual adjust his consumption when he is dissatisfied with his mode of life?

When significant differences in income exist among individuals, those with lower incomes may experience frustration and dissatisfaction. This is especially true when modes of life associated with higher incomes involve consumption patterns that support differences in social position. Position in a status hierarchy may become an element of the individual's self-conception. When this happens, establishing status differences in the eyes of others can become a primary motive in organizing modes of consumption.[4] Under these circumstances, individuals can experience difficulty reconciling their needs with their incomes. Or, put differently, they can experience difficulty in accepting their modes of life.

A mode of consumption that provides satisfaction to the individual can develop over time. At a given time, a mode of consumption consists of certain specific goods. But the definition of a style of life does not restrict it to those goods. Specific components of a mode of consumption can change without doing violence to the consumer's personal identity.

Consumption is a learning process. When we consume a good, we engage in a social practice. By so doing, we better understand the nature of our needs than we did when they only existed as an ideal. I may aspire to own a house because the idea of home ownership has a place in my self-conception. When I actually own a home, I discover new aspects of the reality and of my ideal. This realization may lead me to conclude that the kind of home I own does not really live up to my ideal. As a result, I may sell my house and buy a new one. My need, or at least my understanding of it, changes through the act of consumption. Thus, the learning process associated with consumption can lead to change in the components of the individual's consumption bundle.

The learning process may also lead to the addition of elements not previously included in the set of goods required to realize a mode of consumption. The reality of home ownership brings with it an enrichment of the idea. This can subject the homeowner to any number of additional expenses (gardening equipment, fencing, etc.). The experience of owning a house brings to the consumer an awareness of a set of needs not anticipated during contemplation of the idea. In this sense, the experience of consumption gives birth to new needs.

When a mode of consumption has a potential not fully realized, it acts as a stimulus for change. If we think of listening to recorded music as a social practice, a radio will facilitate that practice, but it will do so in a way noticeably inferior to that made possible by an audio system including a turntable, receiver, tape deck, and speakers. When we watch television, we also participate in a social practice that has various dimensions not all made available to us by a television set. To realize the innate potential of a television, we may also need a video recorder and a cable hookup. As we will see, firms play an important part in discovering hidden dimensions of existing social practices.

If the idea of a mode of life includes the learning process by which individuals experience a widening range of needs implicit in a mode of consumption, then the full realization of a mode of life requires that incomes provide room for expansion of needs. We can allow room for expansion by dividing the individual's income into two parts: that part required to maintain an existing style of life—the committed income—and that part available to support change and development. We will term the latter the consumer's uncommitted income. The division of income into committed and uncommitted parts has important implications for price determination.

To the extent that the individual lives within his income by adopting a mode of life accessible to him given that income, he is likely to use his entire income to support that mode of life. At various levels of income, uncommitted income emerges in two ways. The consumer may give up part of his existing consumption bundle in order to free up income for new items. By doing this, the consumer substitutes the new for the old. Formation of uncommitted income beyond substitution requires the growth of income. In the simplest case, this second part of uncommitted income equals any increase in income over those levels identified with current consumption.

The division of income into committed and uncommitted follows the division of the consumption bundle into those items established within the consumer's mode of consumption and those new items linked to its development. The division of consumer income suggests a division of means of consumption into those already established and those newly introduced. In order to consider price determination, we need to consider the way this distinction constrains price setting on the part of the firm.

Consider a group of consumers with approximately the same levels of income sustaining similar modes of consumption. We will refer to this group as an income-receiving or consumption class. Assume that each consumer within this class has a certain amount of uncommitted income. Assume further that a firm has an idea for a new commodity that fits into the lifestyle of this class, but is not currently part of this class's mode of consumption.

In order to market the new commodity, the firm must make it available to the appropriate class of consumers. To do this, the firm must price the commodity so that its cost to consumers does not exceed their uncommitted income. If a personal computer costs $2,500, then only those consumers who have $2,500 remaining once they have satisfied their established needs can afford to buy one. Thus, the amount of uncommitted income limits the price of the commodity. We will call this limit the uncommitted income constraint.

Obviously, if we define the uncommitted income constraint in this way, it can provide us with only a relatively crude limit to price. Within this limit, price determination depends on two other conditions: the allocation of uncommitted income among new products and competition between firms. We begin with the first of these conditions.

If the uncommitted income constraint is sufficiently large relative to the costs of new commodities, it may allow the consumer to expand his mode of consumption in more than one direction by introducing more than one new good. This means that the consumer must decide on an allocation of his uncommitted income. Consumers' decisions interact with other constraints on the firm (e.g., competition from other firms) to determine the price. Requiring the consumer to allocate his uncommitted income in this way poses problems for our argument since it requires the consumer to set priorities among his potential needs and this setting of priorities tends to blur the distinction between need and preference (the term preference directly implies a ranking of this kind). Some of the considerations that arose in our discussion of impulse in Chapter 1 bear on this issue.

Impulse draws its power from the absence of conscious deliberation. When we consider the prospect of consuming new products, the deliberative process encounters limitations. The most important of these arises because our mode of life does not immediately require consumption of specific new commodities. Based on past experience, the person's integrity does not directly depend on the extension of his mode of consumption in a fixed direction. This introduces an element of indeterminacy into the decision on allocating uncommitted income. Where such indeterminacy exists, deliberation can resolve the issue only up to a point.

One way of dealing with decisions made in such a context is to restrict ourselves to *ex post* description. We know that a consumer prefers x to y because he chooses x over y under conditions where the decision is up to him. This does not mean in any strong sense that the consumer chooses x over y because he prefers it. Nor does it mean that the consumer chooses x over y without reason. It means only that the reasons that drive the consumer do not appear clearly and that deliberation cannot fully resolve the problem posed.

We do not resolve this indeterminacy by introducing a ranking of potential new commodities since an appropriate ranking requires deliberation. Instead, we accept the element of indeterminacy so long as we restrict its range. When we contemplate the introduction of new means of consumption, we evaluate them on the basis of their potential to participate in our mode of life. Because of this, we have explicit criteria to guide us in deliberating among alternatives. While the context for contemplating new commodities restricts deliberation, it does not remove it altogether. Since we can make judgments about the relation of new commodities to our way of life, we can rank new commodities on the basis of those judgments. The resulting ranking can help to explain our preferences.

We do not need new commodities in the same way that we need existing goods. Because of this, we can make judgments between them concerning which fit best into our mode of life. We need the ones that fit better more than we need the ones that fit less well or less directly. In this sense, we can rank potential needs in a way we cannot rank existing needs. By ranking potential needs, we treat them quantitatively rather than qualitatively, relatively rather than absolutely. One result of this is that factors other than need can enter into our decision on how we expand our mode of life. One such factor is price. When firms set prices, they can affect the direction in which modes of consumption develop. As we will see, this reinforces the inverse relation between demand and price.

Now, assume that we have several income classes, each with a different amount of uncommitted income. Some of these income groups may have no use for the new commodity. The remaining groups constitute a pool of potential demand for it. If only one group remains, the price cannot exceed its uncommitted income constraint. If more than one income class remains, the price cannot exceed the uncommitted income constraint of the highest remaining income class. But if more than one income group remains, the extent of the market for the new product will depend on its price, since the price will determine which income classes (or how many of those classes) will have access to the product. If we call the extent of the market (the number of commodities sold at a given price) the demand for the commodity, then an unequal distribution of income can lead to an inverse relationship between demand and price: within limits, the lower the price, the greater the demand.

We will assume that the firm has some information concerning the implications of price for its market, information that it acquires through market research. If the firm concerns itself exclusively with its market, it will set its price according to the lowest uncommitted income constraint. Since, however, the firm sells commodities in order to make profit, the price must both make the commodity available to a consuming class and yield a profit. Whether it does so depends on the costs of production.

The analysis of costs would take us beyond our primary concerns here. Nonetheless, in order to complete our description of the process of price determination, we need to introduce specific assumptions regarding costs. It turns out that we do not need very restrictive assumptions. We can indicate the outline of the problem using two assumptions that are plausible in themselves and gain support from our earlier treatment of production: (1) the cost of producing a unit of output tends to fall as the scale of production increases, and (2) unit costs of production tend to fall over time as the firm has greater experience with the production process and as technical change increases productivity.[5]

The technical specification of the means of production, including its productivity, depends on the know-how available when those means of production were produced. Productivity will vary with the level of technical knowledge. As knowledge develops, productivity increases, and new products and new methods come into existence. Our two assumptions capture in a somewhat idealized way this attribute of production processes that employ produced means of production (i.e., those processes that use wealth to make wealth).

The relationship between cost and demand governs the price of the commodity. We will consider this relationship using two different assumptions concerning income distribution: (1) income is unequally distributed so that a number of income classes exist; (2) income is uniformly distributed so that only one income class exists.

When income is unequally distributed, demand will depend on price. Assume that when the commodity is first introduced, its production cost is lower than the highest uncommitted income constraint, but higher than the next lowest constraint. If the firm sets its price at a level approximately equal to the highest constraint, it will gain access to the greatest number of potential consumers consistent with the condition of profit making. Put differently, it will sell the greatest number of commodities subject to the condition of positive profit. Obviously, if its cost of production exceeds the highest uncommitted income constraint, the commodity cannot be sold at a profit.

By selling the commodity, even if only to a relatively small group of high-income consumers, the firm gains a special advantage. It gains the experience of production and marketing.

According to our second assumption concerning cost, this experience will teach the firm how to produce the commodity more economically, i.e., at a lower unit cost. As unit costs decline over time, the price can be set to make the commodity available to lower income classes, thus expanding the market. According to our first assumption regarding cost, this will further drive unit costs down.

As time passes, we can expect the prices of new commodities to fall and their markets to grow. The implied inverse relationship between demand and price depends crucially on the assumption that incomes are unequally distributed. Indeed, the inverse relation between demand and price has nothing whatsoever to do with consumer choice, but expresses instead the idea of different income classes.

It may seem inconsistent with our earlier analysis of needs to assume that the product will fit into an ever-expanding set of consumption patterns as its price falls. Instead, it may seem more reasonable to assume that different income classes support different modes of consumption that incorporate different commodities. As we suggested above, income classes may correspond to consumption classes. This requires a modification in our analysis of demand and price.

We suggested earlier that costs fall as the market grows because of technical change and economies of scale. A third factor can also play a role. A product can be modified to adapt to different consumption classes. If these modifications result in more and less costly versions of the product, cost will vary with the specific qualities of the product. Less expensive versions of the product can be designed for lower income classes. Pocket calculators can be made out of expensive or cheap materials and can offer different combinations of functions. These versions of the product sell at different prices to different classes of consumers. One effect of this will be to reinforce differences in modes of consumption between different income classes. We can preserve a modified relation between price, demand, and income classes when modes of consumption differ between classes.

Thus far, we have described a dynamic process by which price falls over time as costs fall. By lowering its price, the firm expands its market. What happens when the price of the commodity makes it accessible to the lowest relevant income class?

In order to provide this lowest class with access to its product, the firm sets the price approximately equal to the uncommitted income of that class. To set the price lower would not increase its market; to set it higher would make the product inaccessible. If the firm modifies the product to fit the different lifestyles of different groups, it establishes a set of prices (or a price structure) appropriate simultaneously to the distribution of income and the goal of profit making.

As time passes, we can begin to think of the product as an established part of ongoing modes of consumption. The income spent to acquire it ceases to be uncommitted. Consumers set aside a part of their income for the product. In effect, a need for the commodity has now been established in the mind of the consumer. But given its price, the consumer can buy what he needs of this commodity. In the absence of additional lower income classes, a reduction in price will not increase the market.

In effect, the inverse relation between demand and price tends to disappear for established commodities.[6] More precisely, while a sufficient increase in price can still lower demand, a reduction in price will not significantly increase demand. Furthermore, an increase in price would cause hardship to consumers committed to consuming the product. Originally, when the price was too high for many consumers to afford the product, they simply excluded it from their modes of consumption. They may have suffered envy, but they did not suffer a failure to maintain their modes of life. Now that the price has settled at a level that makes the commodity accessible, the commodity has established a place in the consumer's way of life. If the price rises to a level that makes the product once again inaccessible, the impact on the consumer will be different. He now suffers a failure to support his established way of life.[7]

Thus, the conditions and the implications of price determination differ for new and established commodities. For new commodities, prices have downward flexibility and lower prices will increase demand. For established commodities, a reduction in price will only reduce the firm's profit. These results hold under the assumption that income is unequally distributed. How do price determination and market growth differ when incomes are uniform?

If incomes are unequal, price is governed by the lowest accessible income class. If all relevant consuming classes are accessible given their incomes and given the costs of production, only the uncommitted income constraint of the lowest income class enters into price determination. Thus, even when incomes differ, only one income class acts as an effective constraint on price. This applies directly to the case of uniform income, since in that case only one income class exists. Once the firm establishes the price that makes the commodity accessible to relevant consumers, the entire potential market becomes available. A significantly higher price yields no market; a lower price yields the same market. Thus, a uniform distribution of income does not support an inverse relation between demand and price.

If unequal distribution allows for a group of high-income consumers to experiment with new products, while an equal distribution does not, then inequality encourages the introduction of new products. If, at the outset, a new commodity can only be produced at a high cost, then it can only be sold profitably to high-income consumers. If no high-income consumers exist, the new product has no market and will not be produced. But if the commodity cannot be produced, the experience of production required to lower costs will not be forthcoming. The cost will not fall, the market will not expand, and the producer cannot take advantage of economies of scale. The process that eventually results in wide access to the product never gets started. Under certain assumptions, then, an unequal distribution of income supports the development of new products and of new modes of consumption; and it does so both for low- and for high-income classes. This advantage of unequal distribution depends on the overall amount of wealth available, and the initial costs of production. When enough wealth exists to provide a uniform distribution at a high level and a rate of growth of incomes adequate to support substantial uncommitted incomes, uniform distribution need not impede product innovation.

Nothing in the foregoing suggests that we should consider income inequality desirable in itself, or that we should conclude that only the unequal distribution of income can support the development of new products and modes of consumption. However, the distribution of income can affect the behavior of a market economy in ways relating to the development of modes of consumption.

A surprising result of this analysis concerns the role of cost in price determination. The significant role that cost plays in price determination depends on income inequality. Under a uniform distribution of income, cost determines whether or not the commodity can be produced and sold at the price determined by the uniform uncommitted income constraint; in this sense, cost and income jointly determine price. The wider the range of incomes, the more actively can cost enter into price determination. The greater the number of income groups, the less likely that price will reach a level at which lowering it yields no additional demand.

The fact that consumers make decisions about the allocation of uncommitted income causes firms producing different products to compete for a limited pool of demand. Since consumers' decisions about the direction in which they develop their modes of life can be sensitive to the costs of different alternatives, competition over the pool of uncommitted income reinforces the downward pressure on price associated with a hierarchy of income classes. A third factor comes into play when more than one firm produces a commodity for the same market, or when price determination must take into account the implications of price for entry of new firms. Actual or potential competition can play a decisive role in adjusting price to a level appropriate to exploit fully the market's potential.

The importance of competition emerges clearly when we drop the assumption that firms know the relation of demand to price. Assume that as time passes, costs of production fall and profit margins rise. Even if firms do not know or care about the possibility of market expansion through price reduction, the prospect of competition from other producers targeted at their existing market segment may force them to lower prices.

If firms consider the distribution of sales (demand) among competitors within an industry susceptible to change, and if they consider price an appropriate means to bring about that change, then competition within the industry will limit price and even lead to a fall in prices. Josef Steindl (1952) has analyzed this process in some detail and we only allude to it here. When significant cost advantages accrue to a subset of firms with access to more advanced technology, differences in cost between firms can lead to price competition. Such competition aims at driving out higher cost producers and increasing the market share of those employing the most advanced methods of production. Competition within an industry works with the demand driven process considered above to bring about a decline in price associated with rising productivity.

Price competition helps bring prices into line with productivity and translates increases in productivity into uncommitted income for those consumers whose mode of life incorporates commodities with falling costs and prices. By so doing, price competition helps set in place conditions conducive to product innovation. As we will see in the next section, this process plays a central role in determining the rate of economic growth.

We can distinguish the effects of competition from those of consumer demand by focusing on circumstances in which firms hope to redistribute the pool of demand among themselves rather than increase its overall size. Even though competition may expand that pool, it can proceed with or without awareness of that possibility and achieve it as an unintended consequence. Conditions of demand still govern the eventual outcome with regard to market development.

CAPITAL ACCUMULATION

In a private enterprise economy, consumers can acquire income by selling their labor to firms. Because of this, decisions firms make regarding levels of production, through their impact on employment, will affect the total pool of consumer income, and therefore the demand for the commodities those firms produce. Consumer incomes appear both as a source of demand for commodities and as a cost of production. When we tie income to employment, the scale of production both determines incomes and is determined by incomes.

In order to produce commodities, firms employ capital equipment, labor, and materials. Since it takes time to build a new plant, the amount of capital equipment will be fixed. The firm can still vary its output by varying its degree of capacity utilization. An assembly line can operate at different speeds; capital equipment can be employed continuously or for only limited periods. Different degrees of utilization correspond to different amounts of output. In order to produce more (or less) output with given capital equipment, the firm hires more (or less) labor and uses up more (or fewer) materials.

In practice, firms do not generally know with certainty how much they can sell in a given period, so that when sales volume varies unexpectedly, firms experience unplanned variations in their inventories of produced commodities. Unplanned variations in inventories lead to adjustments in the scale of production and the degree of capacity utilization designed to maintain inventories at the desired level. Assuming such adjustments, it follows that revenues will vary directly with the scale of production. If firms make a profit on each commodity sold, their total profit will vary directly with their levels of production.

While variations in the scale of production can take place with plant and equipment, output can only increase up to a limit defined by the capacity of that equipment. While the definition of full capacity is somewhat complicated, it makes sense to assume that plant and equipment place an upper bound on the scale of production. Thus, within a given period, productive capacity limits profits.

A firm can increase its profit when it is employing all of its productive capacity by increasing its price. So long as the increase in price does not reduce demand, the firm experiences a net gain. But if the increase in price excludes certain groups, demand will suffer.

At a given price, the firm's profit depends on its scale of production, and its scale of production depends on demand. But when consumer incomes depend on the sale of labor to firms, demand will depend on employment, which depends on the scale of production. Thus, demand determines the scale of production, which determines demand.

Revenues from the sale of commodities cover costs of production plus profit. In order to increase their levels of production, firms purchase labor and inputs from other firms. This creates revenues for those firms that cover their costs and also provide them with profits. Thus, the original decision to increase the level of production creates demand equal to the costs of production—wages and the cost of produced inputs. But the revenue created for the firms supplying the inputs also includes profit, which does not correspond to any expenditure associated with producing the inputs needed to meet demand. In effect, the demand directly created by production decisions falls short of the revenue created.

The sum of the costs of production and profit equals the value of the output. Each element of this sum provides a revenue: wages to labor, receipts to those who provide materials, and profits to the firm. Thus, the total value of output equals the revenue created in its production. But the demand created falls short of revenue created by an amount equal to profits. Thus the demand directly generated by production decisions falls short of the total value of output. So long as the prices of commodities include profit, the production of commodities cannot directly create enough demand to buy those commodities.

Even this result depends on the assumption that individuals use their incomes to buy commodities. If consumers save part of their incomes, demand will fall that much farther from the value of output.

When demand falls short of the value of output, a part of that output cannot be sold. Firms will make appropriate adjustments in levels of production to assure equality between sales and output. But so long as profit can be made on the sale of output, demand will continue to fall short of the value of output, and the level of production will seem too high. In fact, of course, the level of production is too low to sustain adequate effective demand; yet the firm perceives the problem in the opposite way: it has produced too much and must lower its level of production. Under these conditions, low levels of production and underutilization of capacity will be the rule. When profit is not spent, demand cannot be maintained at a level adequate to assure employment, consumer incomes, and the utilization of productive capacity.

When the prices of commodities include profit but those who sell the commodities do not spend their profits, a part of the total output cannot be sold. This part corresponds exactly to that amount that does not reappear as demand. This leads us to a striking and important conclusion: Firms can make profits only to the extent that they spend the profit included in the value of output. When firms do not spend profits, they cannot sell a sum of commodities whose value corresponds to the profit they do not spend.

We can put this result in a positive way. The amount of profits that firms realize from the sale of commodities will exactly equal the amount they spend over and above their costs of production (wages and materials costs). In effect, the source of profit is in the decisions firms make to purchase commodities that do not replace used up means of production and labor. As Michal Kalecki (1978) put it, capitalists get what they spend.

If firms use all their profits to buy commodities, and consumers do not save, demand will just equal the value of current output, and firms will realize an amount of profit on current sales of commodities exactly equal to the amount realized in the past. If consumer saving takes place such that the sum of consumer expenditures on the products of firms falls short of the sum of their incomes from the sale of their labor to firms, then demand associated with current revenues will fall short of the value of the products corresponding to those revenues. To maintain demand, firms must spend not only their profits, but also an amount equal to net saving of consumers. That is, firms must want to spend more than they earned in profits, and by an amount equal to consumer savings. In order to do so, firms borrow an amount from consumers equal to their net savings.

Firms can spend profits in two ways. First they can distribute profits to shareholders, who treat profits as income and use them to maintain a mode of consumption. If the shareholders do not save, they, in effect, spend the firm's profits for it, and thereby assure that demand equals the value of output. Second, firms can retain their profits to acquire more capital. By accumulating capital, firms increase their productive capacity. Thus, by using profits to increase their capital investments, firms establish a basis for making more profit in the future.

In a private enterprise system, individual consumers own firms and use their profits as a source of income. It does not follow that firms view their profits essentially as a source of income for shareholders. When we think about a private enterprise economy, we can think of a system oriented either to producing incomes for the owners of capital or to generating profit for investment. Normally, the second view accords best with the history and logic of private enterprise. The system does create substantial incomes for those who own capital, but the provision of incomes is not the firm's primary objective.[8] Success for the firm generally means reserving a part of profits or "retained earnings" for investment. In the following, we will treat distributed earnings to shareholders as the passive element in the life of the firm, and focus attention on the relation between profits and investment.

To summarize: the production and the sale of commodities generates revenues for consumers in the form of wages, salaries, and distributed earnings. If we assume that consumers spend these revenues in maintaining their modes of consumption, demand will still fall short of the value of output by an amount equal to retained earnings. If consumers save, the amount of the shortfall will equal the sum of retained earnings and savings.

The classical economists (including Marx) assumed that profits were automatically used to acquire additional capital equipment. This assumption was supported by two others: First, the classical economists assumed, as we have, that capital accumulation is the primary motive for the firm. Second, they assumed that capital equipment was the only form of investment. Thus, retained earnings could not be used to acquire financial assets (stocks and bonds), but had to be used to buy commodities (means of production). This constraint would assure that demand equals the value of aggregate output.

The neoclassical theory arrives at the same result, but takes a different route. It introduces a mechanism for adjusting savings (including retained earnings) to investment. This mechanism requires that firms vary their investment plans according to variations in the rate of interest, and that consumers also vary their savings decisions according to variations in the rate of interest. When this mechanism works, investment will absorb savings, assuring equality of effective demand with the value of output at full capacity.

The Keynesian theory differs from both the classical and neoclassical. Rather than assuming that investment depends either on the amount of revenue currently coming into the firm or on the rate of interest, modern Keynesian theories emphasize the part played by the firm's expectations of profitability. Since the purpose of investment is to increase the firm's profit, the idea that expected profitability will determine investment makes sense.

When we suggest that firms make investment decisions based on profit expectations, we assume that firms have the kind of information about the future they require to form expectations. Much depends on whether we think that the environment within which firms function has sufficient stability to support predictions about the future. We need not assume that agents can make predictions with anything like certainty, but we do need to assume that the future will not differ so dramatically from the past so as to make information based on past experience irrelevant to expectations about the future.

Consider the demand for particular commodities. If we think that this demand depends on consumer preferences, we have no reason to assume that it will not change radically from period to period as "tastes" change. An economic environment in which demand depends on individual preferences or tastes need not support the kind of reasonable expectations about the future required for investment decisions. Obviously, nothing in the concept of preference as employed in neoclassical economics directly requires that tastes change. Nonetheless, if we invoke the idea of arbitrary preferences, we must consider recurrence of wants equally arbitrary. Recurrence of a particular structure of demand happens by accident.

The idea of need has implications for expectations different from those of preference. When demand depends on need, firms have every reason to consider the past a worthwhile, if inexact, source of information about the future. Needs depend on personality structures that endure through time and change in rational (to some degree predictable) patterns. Dependence of demand on needs encourages the stability required for the formation of expectations.

Assuming that the economic and social environment encourages firms to form expectations about the future profitability of an investment plan, we can distinguish two cases. In the first case, firms assume that the future will be just like the past, and form investment plans accordingly. In the second case, firms assume that the future will be much like the past, but may differ from it in certain important ways. These two cases correspond to two fundamentally different views regarding the nature of a market economy.

Under case one, firms make investment decisions based on past experience of profitability. If they have experienced high levels of profit in the past, they will expect current investment to yield high levels of profit in the future. Thus, high levels of profit encourage high rates of investment. But if many firms share this experience, the overall level of investment and rate of economic growth will be high. This high level of investment will in turn generate high levels of profit, thereby verifying those expectations based on past experience. If profits have been robust, and firms assume that the future will reproduce the past, they will act to assure that profits will continue to be robust. Of course, the same circle of causation works when profits are low. In this case profitability discourages investment, so that the circle of causation works to reproduce low levels of profit and investment. Without investment, demand and profitability cannot revive, and low levels of production and profit continue.

The mutual determination of investment and profit means that, in a sense, a private enterprise economy grows as rapidly as it "wants" to. Following Joan Robinson (1962), we will refer to the self-sustaining expansion of the economy as "desired growth." Investment plans depend on expectations of profitability that depend on the vitality of past investment. Thus, if many firms develop (for whatever reason), a sudden enthusiasm for investment, they can shift the economy onto a higher plane of self-sustaining growth and profitability. No doubt this can happen only within certain limits. But unless the economy normally operates at its limits—full-capacity production with maximum feasible prices and profit margins—the idea of desired growth comes into play.

While the system of firms can shift itself to a higher (or lower) plane of profits and investment simply by desiring to do so, no individual firm can raise its profits simply by increasing investment. Decisions made by other firms constrain its actions. Those decisions generate a level of demand that determines the profitability of the particular producer and thus his particular investment plans. No individual firm can increase its market by increasing its level of investment, nor can it grow more rapidly by simply desiring to do so.

In a private enterprise economy, firms do not act in concert but on the basis of private ends and separate strategies for accumulation. The idea that the system of firms could desire to grow more rapidly does not make sense. If individual firms acted as though their desire to grow more rapidly could create a market sufficient to justify their accelerating growth, their joint efforts would facilitate that result. If firms could grow without regard to their markets, the market would justify their growth; but they can't and it doesn't.

In order to break this circle of causation, we must modify our assumption regarding expectations. If instead of assuming that the future will be just like the past, firms assume that the future, while much like the past, can also differ from it, then an individual firm might raise its own rate of investment to a higher level even though its experience of demand in the past does not justify such an increase.

When a firm increases its rate of investment, it burdens itself with additional productive capacity in the future. What could lead a firm to believe that demand in the future will reach levels requiring that capacity, when demand is not currently growing rapidly enough to reach such levels? What might convince the firm that the circumstances determining demand are changing in such a way to justify a change in its investment plans?

Our analysis of price determination can prove helpful in answering this question. There we argued that when the current price of a commodity makes it inaccessible to certain income classes, a price reduction will increase demand. When falling costs allow for such a reduction, the firm can anticipate and change the circumstances determining demand for its product. Thus, for those firms producing products whose markets can expand to incorporate new classes of consumers, demand can grow more rapidly in the future than it has in the past.

If a firm only produces commodities whose markets lack this potential, its investment plans will be determined by the rate at which demand had grown in the past, which depends on the overall growth of the economy. As the economy grows, the demand for labor increases, new workers are hired, and new consumers are created. These new consumers can purchase the firm's product, so that market saturation need not mean a market fixed in size. The firm's market will, however, grow at a rate more or less equal to that of the economy as a whole. The determinants of desired growth determine the firm's rate of growth.

The firm can break this limit only by producing a commodity whose demand is not circumscribed by the overall growth rate of the economy. If the firm does not already produce such a commodity, it must find one. Thus by innovating (undertaking to find and introduce new commodities), the firm refuses to be limited by the current rate of overall economic growth.

What happens when large numbers of firms undertake innovation in the hopes of expanding their markets at a rate more rapid than the current overall rate of market growth? The demand-creating effects of investment associated with innovation will catapult the economy onto a higher plane of growth. In this way, the growth of the economy depends on the ability of firms to introduce and develop new products. This ability, in turn, depends on the economy's potential to absorb new products.

In a rapidly growing economy, various factors conspire to support continuing rapid growth. High profits resulting from rapid growth sustain expectations of profitability, which encourage high levels of investment. The rapidly expanding market leads to diminishing costs of production, allowing firms to widen access to their commodities by lowering prices (at least relative to wages). The resulting market expansion further stimulates investment and economic growth. Rapid growth supports the creation of uncommitted incomes in two ways: (1) It increases real incomes of currently employed workers by lowering the prices of commodities they consume (relative to their wages); (2) It requires hiring of new workers and brings new consumption bundles into existence. Thus, various factors that cause rapid growth also result from rapid growth.

The private enterprise market economy has an inherent dynamism. When we allow innovation to support the expectation that future profitability will differ from past profitability, the profit-oriented firm will vigorously pursue changes in methods of production and modes of consumption that will underwrite its future profitability. Thus, the pursuit of profit acts as a tremendous stimulus to the development of modes of consumption. Nothing in the foregoing implies that only the profit motive can do this work in society; but historically, the pursuit of profit has had a unique ability to bring about economic development and the transformation of modes of consumption. The investigation of this ability has been the central concern of economists as diverse in their approaches as Smith, Marx, and Schumpeter.

The market supports the individual's right to determine his own mode of consumption. But for the market to provide for individual needs, the inherent dynamism of individual consumption must be matched by dynamism on the side of the producer. Profit provides the needed dynamic insofar as it drives the firm to seek out and introduce new commodities. For capital accumulation to sustain itself, needs must change and develop. Yet it is the process of accumulation on the part of the particular firm that provides an ever-changing mix of products capable of satisfying continually changing modes of consumption.

The formation and provision of social needs as discussed in Chapter 1 may require a market based in impersonal exchange and units of production oriented toward profit making and accumulation. To avoid this result we must assume that society has sufficient wealth to satisfy individual needs. The profit motive and impersonal exchange presuppose firms oriented toward private accumulation and production for the market, and consumers who have money incomes that they employ to acquire the products of those firms. Does the provision of social need also require private ownership of capital and that consumer incomes be tied to the sale of their labor to firms? In our final chapter we will consider this question. It turns out that both parts of this question involve the issues of individual rights in the economy and the economy's ability to satisfy individual needs.

PRIVATE 5
ENTERPRISE

INCOME FROM PROPERTY

Consider an economy in which all means of consumption and all
means of production are privately owned.[1] Consumers own particular goods that they use to satisfy needs. They also hold money
and possibly shares in particular firms. Firms own means of production, which they use to produce commodities for sale to other firms
or to consumers. Firms produce and sell commodities in order to
make profits, part of which they distribute to their shareholders and
part of which they retain for investment in capital expansion. In
order to produce commodities, firms also hire consumers (i.e., as
workers) and pay them wages or salaries.

In this economy, when an individual needs to acquire a good,
he must buy it from its owner with money. Usually, goods that consumers need but do not own will be owned by the firms that
produce them. If consumers need goods whose cost exceeds the
amount of money they have, their need for goods becomes a need
for money. Since all wealth is privately owned, individuals have two
primary sources of money available to them: dividends due to the
owners of firms, and wages (or salaries) paid in exchange for labor.
In the economy we are considering, all income comes from the
ownership of property (property in capital or property in labor), and
ultimately from capital either as a claim over part of its revenue
(dividends) or in exchange for part of its revenue (wages).

The fact that all income comes from capital makes some sense if
we bear in mind that capital produces the means of consumption
purchased with that income. In effect, when they purchase labor

and distribute part of their earnings to shareholders, firms create the incomes used to purchase their products. Since only firms produce means of consumption, their ability to produce should act as a constraint on the purchasing power of consumers.

The requirement that income come from property has other implications. When income depends on property, the amount and kind of property the individual owns will determine the amount of income he receives. It follows that the mode of consumption the individual attains will depend on his property

The income that individuals receive from ownership of capital will depend on the amount of stock they hold and the profitability of the particular firms whose shares they own. With a well-developed market in shares, the individual's income from capital can also be made to depend on the outcome of speculation: the skill with which he buys low and sells high, and the good or bad fortune that befalls the stock he owns.

Income from the sale of labor will depend on its market value. If laborers offer different kinds of labor that sell in different markets and at different prices, then income from the sale of labor can vary from person to person. Variation in incomes is inevitable in a society that attaches income to property and therefore makes income depend on attributes of particular markets, especially a market valuation of particular kinds of labor.

Variations in income associated with differences in the kind of property (including the kind of labor) held by different individuals provide the basis for a hierarchy of wealth and status, expressed also as a hierarchy of modes of life. Thus, when we link income to property, we establish a rule for need satisfaction: satisfaction of needs will depend on and vary with the ownership of property.

What argument could we give to support the idea that need satisfaction should be determined in this way? One argument rests on the link between private property and a particular conception of individual freedom. Assume that individual freedom means that the individual enters into social relations exclusively at his will. This implies that rights precede the social order and adhere to people outside of society. This assumption disconnects rights from any idea of a person that must be realized in a particular sort of society.[2] It leads to the conclusion that a social order should work to serve (or preserve) the individual's presocial autonomy. The relation of a person to his property comes before his relationship to others.

In a pure private enterprise economy, where all income derives from property, relations between individuals occur through their property. The only way in which a source of income other than property could emerge would involve the appropriation of property from some individuals and its transfer to others. If we introduce a government into a private enterprise economy, we get just this result. The government acts as a source of income by appropriating the incomes of some individuals (i.e., through taxation), and transferring it to others. The legitimacy of the government acting as a source of income rests on the presence of certain social obligations that take precedence over the use of property in the pursuit of private ends. In the absence of such obligations, private ends govern the use of all property.

Consider two individuals, each endowed with a particular kind of labor. For the moment, we leave aside matters involving the way in which such endowments are acquired. If one individual happens to be a librarian and the other a lawyer, then in a pure private enterprise economy their respective incomes will depend on the situation in the markets for librarians and for lawyers. This difference in income would be justified as follows: the librarian owns his skill, knowledge, and aptitude, as does the lawyer. Firms looking for librarians or lawyers own the money they have to spend. All property owners are free to use their property to achieve their private ends. If such use involves firms paying more to lawyers than to librarians, then it would violate a firm's property rights, and therefore subvert its freedom, to stop it from doing so. Any intrusion into the market that imposes a rate of exchange independent of the wills of the parties to the transactions undermines the freedom of the property owner to dispose of his property as he sees fit—that is, to achieve his private ends.

An obvious question arises concerning the idea that the firm is a property owner in pursuit of a private end. We can get around this problem in a private enterprise economy if we can think of the firm working for the private ends of its owners—making a profit for them.[3] If we impose a rate of exchange that favors the librarian or the lawyer, we in effect appropriate part of the wealth due to the owners of the firm and transfer it to those selling their services to the firm. If we allow the free market to operate, then we would expect an exchange that is advantageous to both parties. If such an exchange yields a greater income to the lawyer than to the librarian, that difference is embedded in respect for property rights and individual freedom.

If the lawyer makes a substantially higher income, he gains access to modes of life unavailable to the librarian. Beyond this opportunity to maintain a style of life, the lawyer's income may allow him the opportunity to invest in shares. The lawyer can now use his income to acquire more income, while the librarian uses his income to maintain a modest lifestyle.

By investing his income, the lawyer has taken the first step on the road to real wealth. In a private enterprise economy, significant accumulations of wealth result from capital investment. Private ownership of capital has two important implications: (1) it creates significant differences in income and wealth, and (2) it makes possible the use of wealth to create more wealth.

While our librarian works hard to maintain a modest lifestyle, our lawyer works hard to become wealthy. Becoming wealthy in a private enterprise economy depends less on whether you work hard, and more on what you work hard at. We can distinguish several cases, each corresponding to a particular personality structure and life-experience.

1. *The superior-acquisitive personality:* Certain individuals work hard to make money; they devote themselves to the work of becoming wealthy. When they succeed, they do so in part precisely because they have devoted themselves to money-making, and in part because of good fortune along the way. When they fail, their failure is not due to laziness, but to bad fortune or lack of talent. The superior-acquisitive personality who remains poor does so because he is unlucky or untalented (we may or may not want to consider talent also a matter of luck).

2. *The inferior-acquisitive personality:* Some individuals need wealth just as much as superior-acquisitive personalities do, but will not work hard for it. For an acquisitive personality, the inability to work hard is in the nature of a character flaw. It stems, perhaps, from a sense of inferiority associated with a deep-seated fear of success. Inferior-acquisitive personalities have little chance of becoming wealthy. Whatever chance they have requires luck; either they inherit wealth, or they happen on it (e.g., by winning the lottery). The wealthy inferior-acquisitive personality has the good fortune of finding the wealth he would not devote himself to making.

3. *The virtuous personality:* Individuals who have a vocation that provides income according to the value of their services in the market posses a virtuous personality. Their income satisfies them if they can afford a lifestyle consistent with their vocations. They are less concerned with making money than with the quality of their work and its intrinsic rewards. The virtuous personality may succeed or fail in his vocation. Just as in the case of the superior-acquisitive personality, success or failure will depend on luck and talent.

A private enterprise economy rewards hard work, what the individual works hard at, luck, and talent. It does so by valuing labor in the market and providing, in the ownership of capital, a vehicle for money-making. Private enterprise supports a hierarchy of wealth and status based on the link between income and property. The position of an individual within this hierarchy will depend on two considerations. First, his personality determines the position he aspires to and his ability to work hard to attain that position. Second, his life experience determines whether he happens to be well placed to succeed in his aspirations. One important component of life experience is good or bad fortune (e.g., inheritance).

An important subset of the individuals in a private enterprise economy (especially personality types 1 and 3) acquire as much wealth as they need. Indeed, their need determines the amount of wealth they acquire. In a private enterprise economy, the need for wealth does not imply any right to wealth. Given that it encourages the acquisitive personality, private enterprise could hardly support any individual's right to the things he needs. However, in a private enterprise economy, each individual is free to do what he can to acquire the things he needs so long as he does so by using and acquiring property. In effect, under private enterprise, the individual is free to satisfy his needs, but he has no right to do so.

CAPITALIST AND RENTIER

Private ownership of capital contributes to individual freedom when freedom requires a right to devote yourself to the work of becoming wealthy. Private enterprise allows and encourages the superior-acquisitive personality to express itself fully through a distinct mode of life. This mode of life centers around the need to acquire wealth. What does it mean to need wealth?

First, my need for wealth may be a need for useful objects capable of satisfying specific needs. I invest my money so that it will yield a profit, or make money for me. I use the profit to enhance my mode of consumption. Thus, capital investment may help me to overcome dissatisfaction with my lifestyle. As we noted earlier, dissatisfaction may be linked to the existence of a hierarchy of wealth and status. I need to make money in order to move up in this hierarchy. In order to make money, I need access to capital.

Beyond the particular goods and lifestyle wealth affords me, however, I may want wealth for its own sake; that is, I may identify with the idea of being wealthy, so that the work of becoming wealthy becomes a part of my idea of who I am. The process of making wealth, or becoming ever more wealthy, has become a component of my personality structure. In this case, the particular goods I can and do acquire with my wealth have less significance than the amount of wealth that I own. Indeed, the importance of certain specific goods (diamonds and furs, for example) will stem less from their utility than from their cost.

We use the term "capitalist" to describe those individuals for whom the process of acquiring wealth takes on importance in itself. The capitalist expresses his personality through accumulation. The successful capitalist exemplifies the superior-acquisitive personality, although, as we will see later, he may well harbor a virtuous soul within his acquisitive shell. The capitalist's purpose is to build an empire that bears the stamp of his person, and may even carry his name (e.g., Ford Motor Company). He owns his capital and makes that capital (together with any additional capital he can acquire) provide the basis for his social recognition.

The rentier occupies an opposing pole to the capitalist. He owns capital (stocks and bonds) and acquires income from its ownership, but he has no interest in subordinating his personality to the well-being of his capital (i.e., he does not want to work for a living). If the rentier acquires his wealth by inheritance, he exemplifies the lucky inferior-acquisitive personality. If he acquires his wealth as a reward for hard work undertaken in his youth, he exemplifies the superior-acquisitive personality gone bad. Perhaps he never really was devoted to hard work, and gave it up as soon as possible. We might call him the not-so-superior-acquisitive personality.

For the rentier, capital provides the means by which he acquires the goods that satisfy his individual needs. Like the capitalist, these needs do not include the need to become wealthier. For the rentier, capital is nothing more than a source of income. The rentier's personal identity includes a position in a social hierarchy, and he needs the income from capital to maintain that position. But making wealth, and the pursuit of increasingly larger accumulations of wealth, are not components of his personality structure.

The rentier uses his capital for personal ends. To this extent, he preserves the integrity of his personality, and does not allow his capital to dominate his life. By contrast, the capitalist tends to be preoccupied with his capital and its well-being. The capitalist risks losing himself in his capital by subordinating his personal needs to the needs of his enterprise.[4] He works long hours, expending his time and energy to make his capital thrive rather than developing his personality—his intellectual faculties, his appreciation for the arts, his general knowledge, etc. His one-dimensional existence molds to his one-dimensional personality, and obstructs the growth of a multifaceted mode of life.

The capitalist and the rentier differ in two important respects. First, the capitalist has a vocation: he works for a living, the rentier does not. Second, the capitalist identifies himself (including his personality) with his capital: the rentier does not.

But the idea of a vocation does not necessarily imply a personal identification with a particular enterprise. We can use the term entrepreneur to describe the vocation of the capitalist. If we can think of the entrepreneur as pursuing his vocation without necessarily owning his capital, then this has important implications for the private ownership of capital. In particular, it calls into question the link between private enterprise and entrepreneurship.

Entrepreneurship viewed as a vocation is akin to being a dentist. The individual who adopts the vocation gains satisfaction from it, and especially from doing it well. The vocation requires energy, skill, knowledge, and hard work. Some who adopt the vocation are better at it than others. We can estimate the dentist's success in his vocation by the well-being of his patients and by the quality of his workmanship in drilling teeth, fitting crowns, etc. The dentist's success does not depend on owning his equipment, or on the rate of profit he makes if he does own his equipment. If the dentist owns his facilities, he may also hire others to work for him: receptionists, hygienists, even other dentists. He may open up and administer a dental clinic, then use the profits from his clinic to finance a string of clinics. If he does, he moves from being a dentist to being a capitalist.

Just as the vocation of dentist requires access to certain equipment, the vocation of entrepreneur requires access to capital. But to be an entrepreneur do you also need to own capital and make yourself rich by making your capital grow? Must an entrepreneur, unlike a dentist, also be a capitalist?

The successful entrepreneur requires knowledge and skill in particular areas: finance, marketing, management—especially as they bear on the specific products his firm produces. To be an entrepreneur is to exercise that skill. Exercise of that skill requires the use of capital, but not necessarily its ownership. In the modern corporation, "the entrepreneur" functions as the many people with specialized knowledge—the entrepreneur is now the financial analyst, the market analyst, the manager, the accountant, the economist, etc. Each individual specialist has a vocation he can exercise without owning capital.

If entrepreneurship is a vocation (the true vocation of the capitalist), then it is also a proper mode of life for the virtuous personality. Entrepreneurship reveals the virtuous soul of the superior-acquisitive personality of the capitalist.

Modern economic organization drives a wedge between the condition of ownership and the work of producing wealth and profit. Our conviction (if such exists) that production of wealth and profit are important to society's well-being no longer directly implies the necessity of private ownership of capital.

When individuals own shares in the corporation, the corporation becomes so much privately owned capital. Since the corporation distributes part of its earnings to its shareholders, we might be tempted to conclude that profit making is a goal imposed on the firm by its shareholders. It works for its owner's private ends. This conclusion plays an important part in the argument for the justness of the distribution of income according to the ownership of property (especially property in capital).

An alternative argument also makes sense. The firm may engage in profit-making activities for reasons unrelated to the particular needs of its owners. Individuals who own shares buy and sell them at will. They do not invest their personalities (and private ends) into their shares, or into the firm represented by those shares. The only private end the firm serves for the shareholder is the general one of making him wealthier.

The firm's purpose (profit making) does not change when shares change hands (that is, when ownership changes). We might think of this as an institutional purpose built into an organizational structure. Changes in ownership and even in management leave the twin goals of profit making and capital accumulation unaffected.

We are now in a better position to separate out certain of the critical components of private enterprise, and see which require private ownership:

1. *The capitalist* identifies himself with his enterprise and devotes himself to its well-being. For the capitalist, the active pursuit of wealth is an essential component of his personality.

2. *The entrepreneur* identifies himself with his vocation—making capital grow—rather than with any particular enterprise. He can work for different firms without losing his sense of self. He can also specialize in one of the skilled trades that make up entrepreneurship: accountant, manager, etc.

3. *The rentier's* vocation is consumption; he needs capital exclusively as a source of income. He must own capital, but he does

not commit his personality to the activities associated with making capital grow. The position in society that the revenue from his capital affords him is an essential component of his personality.

4. *The corporation* pursues accumulation and profit making more for its own reasons (perhaps simply because that is what it does and how it defines itself), and not because particular owners require it to do so.

Of these four elements of private enterprise, only the first and third clearly require private ownership of capital. The importance of private ownership of capital stems from the way in which it allows individuals to incorporate the idea of wealth into their personalities. Private ownership has importance to the capitalist because his capital provides him with a purpose and a sense of identity. Private ownership has importance to the rentier because it allows him to pursue a lifestyle that expresses his position in a social hierarchy. For the capitalist, the work of becoming wealthy is a determining element of his personality structure. For the rentier, relative position in a social hierarchy is a determining element of his personality structure. In effect, private enterprise is a way of life (actually, two ways of life): the ways of life of the acquisitive personality.

At this point we could, of course, introduce value judgments regarding either the modes of life themselves, or the qualities of the social-economic system needed to support those modes of life. For example, if we value equality, we may find it lamentable that private enterprise enables small numbers of individuals to acquire disproportionate amounts of wealth and use that wealth to support lifestyles that emphasize their relative social position. Alternatively, we might consider hierarchies of wealth desirable because we believe that by stimulating envy, they create incentives that lead to individual efforts that contribute to the growth of social wealth. How can we fruitfully address issues such as this?

In our discussion of private enterprise, we emphasized the relation between private ownership of capital and individual personality structure. Private enterprise corresponds to specific individual needs and modes of life. It encourages acquisitiveness and the work of self-aggrandizement. It would cease to be viable if individuals gave up their concern with the acquisition of wealth and with their place in a social hierarchy of wealth. Given this starting point, we can make some preliminary judgments about private enterprise by considering the implications of the acquisitive mode of life.

Among the most basic questions we could ask are those having to do with the modes of life themselves. Does the pursuit of wealth or of relative position in a hierarchy of wealth provide an adequate basis for personality development? Or do they stunt the growth of the individual and impede his efforts to find a satisfactory sense of personal identity? Do the modes of life associated with private enterprise place strains on the individual that make it difficult or impossible to realize his mode of life and satisfy his needs?[5]

Obviously, economic analysis cannot answer these questions. Nonetheless, the questions have fundamental implications for any judgment we might make about the viability of private enterprise. If private enterprise places too great a strain on those individuals who best express its distinctive purposes and unique virtues, we cannot consider it a viable way of organizing society.

If capitalists come to expect more from life than long days devoted to making their capital grow, if they develop a sense of self broader than the one expressed strictly through their enterprises, if they develop the need to realize a many-sided personality development, then they cease to be very good capitalists. They may very well maintain a commitment to some aspect of the entrepreneurial vocation. But if the demands of that vocation begin to absorb their lives, this will place a strain on their personalities.

The greater the emphasis society places on self-expression and self-development, the greater the dissatisfaction and frustration experienced by those who devote their lives to making (rather than using) wealth. The more society emphasizes consumption as a mode of self-expression, the more time the individual must devote to using rather than making wealth, making the mode of life of the capitalist less satisfying. The capitalist's way of life will become more and more a way of acquiring the wealth the individual will later devote himself to using. Capitalism's success in producing social wealth, and thereby providing individuals with access to a wide range of modes of consumption, is based on its encouragement of the superior-acquisitive personality. That same success tends to lessen the satisfaction that the superior-acquisitive personality gains from his mode of life by highlighting its parochialism and the lack of self-development associated with it.

A second group of questions falls more narrowly within the scope of economic analysis. These questions examine the implications of the acquisitive mode of life for the functioning of a market economy. Obviously, private enterprise requires markets. How does it affect the way in which they function? In part, this is also a question of viability. Does private enterprise contribute to the reproduction and growth of social wealth, or does it impede it by disorganizing market institutions? Economic analysis can also consider the necessity of private ownership of capital in relation to the reproduction and development of social wealth. Are the motives that drive the acquisitive modes of life necessary to support the market? Must we have a market if we are to satisfy individual needs?

In earlier chapters we suggested that the answer to this last question depends on the kinds of needs individuals have and the limits to the expansion of wealth. In particular, it depends on the inevitability that individual needs expand through time. Expansion of needs results from the presence of a hierarchy of modes of life that stimulates envy and the need for more wealth as a means of advancement within that hierarchy. In the final section of this chapter we consider the relationship between private enterprise and hierarchies of social status.

A final question concerning private enterprise brings us closer to matters of moral judgement: Does the individual have a right to own capital? This is the most important question, because it takes us back to the obligations society has to respect the integrity of the individual. In the concluding section of this chapter, and in the epilogue, we take up the question of individual rights within the economy.

PRIVATE ENTERPRISE AND PRIVATE PROPERTY

We can trace many of the distinctive characteristics of the modern market economy to the fact that individuals do not have sufficient wealth to satisfy their needs. Economists use the term scarcity to describe a situation in which certain needs go unsatisfied (due either to the amount of wealth or to its distribution). While our analysis of the market economy does not lean heavily on the idea of scarcity, we do stress the importance of enabling the individual to decide how he will satisfy his needs, and possibly which needs he will satisfy. Why should a situation arise in which individual needs go unsatisfied?

The logic of the market rests on change in, and especially expansion of, needs. This multiplication of needs tends to assure that, at any given point in time, certain needs—especially new needs—will go unsatisfied. Thus, an economy's failure to satisfy needs originates in the encouragement it gives to the expansion of needs. "Scarcity" results from this process of expansion. When the economic process incorporates change and development, the economy participates in the work of creating needs it cannot satisfy. It does this by creating a need for wealth and by supporting acquisitive modes of life. The modes of life we identify with private enterprise will, given a supportive environment, assure the development of hierarchies of wealth, the pursuit of wealth as a means for enhancing the individual's relative social position, and the need for ever-greater accumulations of wealth.[6]

When needs go unsatisfied, two results can follow. Either the individual gives up his freedom to determine what needs he will satisfy and to pursue the acquisition of the wealth he needs, or the individual gives up his right to satisfy his needs.

Whether we give up our right to the things we need depends on whether we defend our right to own capital. If our right to property does not extend to capital, we will be unable to act on our need for wealth and for the position in the social hierarchy that wealth affords us. The freedom to pursue wealth means very little if we are not allowed the means to make ourselves wealthy. Thus, we can go some way toward answering the question of whether we have a right to the things we need by first answering the question: Do we have a right to own capital? If we have no right to own capital, it does not immediately follow that we do have a right to the things that we need, but it does encourage us in that direction.[7]

If we have a right to own capital, that right must follow from our right to own property in general. But the fact that we have the right to own property does not directly imply that we have a right to own capital. We must first have some idea of what kinds of things can be rightfully appropriated; obviously, some cannot. We cannot claim property rights over another person (we do not have the right to own slaves merely because we have the right to own property). Even if we can afford it, we do not have the right to own a nuclear missile.

Private enterprise economies tend to support few restrictions on ownership. You can buy and sell almost anything. Yet, the few restrictions that remain indicate the application of criteria concerning legitimate appropriation. Why am I denied the right to own a nuclear missile? The answer to this must have to do with the idea that I could have no legitimate use for a nuclear missile. Whether I have the right to own a handgun follows the same criterion. Even if we consider the killing of defenseless animals (hunting) a legitimate use for a weapon, handguns are generally considered inappropriate to that purpose. The only legitimate use for handguns (aside from collecting) is self-defense. One argument in the debate over gun control centers on the usefulness of handguns in self-defense. However the debate comes out, the issue of legitimate use plays an important part.

We have taken a large step here and should acknowledge the absence of any real argument for it. We cannot deduce from the examples of nuclear missiles or handguns that certain things cannot be rightfully owned unless we demonstrate that the laws against ownership of missiles or guns are just laws that do not themselves violate individual rights. We can, however, point out that in thinking about property we must also consider the things that can be property. The way we resolve this matter bears on a whole set of questions associated with the idea of a just distribution.

If we accept the idea developed in Chapter 2 that objects have socially objective uses defined within social practices, then the idea of legitimate use makes sense since it refers to objective properties rather than subjective states. From a purely subjective standpoint, the uses, for example, of a handgun are not intrinsically legitimate or illegitimate. Use depends on the particular intent of the person with the gun. The idea of objective use not only plays a role in our treatment of demand and price determination, it also plays a part in our thinking concerning the limits of property ownership. This approach has much in common with one of the approaches to property rights discussed in Chapter 2: the one that justifies property right on the basis of integration into a mode of life. We can apply this idea to the ownership of capital by asking whether the individual can integrate capital into his mode of life and, in that sense, attach it to his person.[8]

The idea of legitimate use can also be interpreted differently. Considering the examples we have employed, we may want to think of legitimate use as a use that does not infringe on the rights of others.[9] If my only use for a handgun is to shoot innocent people, and thereby violate their rights, making ownership of handguns illegal only eliminates my right to violate the rights of others. This argument seems to be involved in a government's assertion that it has built up an arsenal of nuclear weapons for "defensive" purposes.

We can reconcile the requirement that the good be incorporated into a mode of life with the requirement that its consumption be consistent with respect for the rights of others only by restricting modes of life—and therefore personal identities—to those that incorporate the idea of respect for the integrity of others. Practically, the two requirements may have different implications when modes of life exist that do not accord with the idea of mutual respect. When we link legitimate use to the idea of respect for the rights of others, we have a standard for explaining the proper scope of the market, but this standard is ideal rather than empirical. If, for example, society deems certain drugs illegal for reasons having nothing to do with any danger to rights traceable to their use, then those drugs have a legitimate use even though society does not recognize it as such.

Defining possible ways of life for people and setting the limits within which people define their own ways of life is the essence of a coherent social order. We use terms such as custom and culture to connote the process of defining ways of life insofar as they have historically contingent aspects, and insofar as they involve concrete details of daily life. We use terms such as ethical and just to connote a more universal social definition of ways of life, a definition that is not historically contingent and that allows broad scope to individual self-determination in setting the concrete content of ways of life.

The ethical aspect involves a claim regarding the consistency of modes of life with the concept of a person. This claim presupposes the possibility of objective judgment. Obviously, such a claim is not self-evident. Since we do not explicitly argue for it here, we con- sider it as a presupposition. Arguments in support of this claim have their roots in Kant's moral imperative and Hegel's idea of an ethical order. Our own argument has a closer affinity with Hegel than with Kant in requiring that moral imperatives be concretized within a determinate structure of social relations.[10]

Before pursuing the analysis of legitimate use, we should emphasize a point that might otherwise go unnoticed. Both criteria of legitimate use apply to the individual and his personal needs. Neither says anything about whether society (in some sense of the term) benefits by the individual's use of the object. Thus, if we allow private ownership of capital, society may benefit from the work of capitalists in building an industrial-commercial infrastructure, or it may suffer because of the inequities and insecurities attendant on hierarchies of wealth and power. Our criteria do not take either of these possible outcomes directly into account. Instead, they focus on the individual's property rights. On this basis, we can try to say something about private ownership over capital by asking whether the individual has a legitimate use for capital.

This question is difficult to answer mainly because it leads us in different directions depending on whether we focus on the capitalist or the rentier. The rentier needs to own capital in order to accomplish certain private ends (mainly to make himself, or keep himself, rich). But while he needs to own capital, the rentier does not use it himself. He lets others use it to make money for him. In no reasonable sense can the rentier be thought to integrate his capital into his mode of consumption. He cannot impress his personality on his capital and give it a meaning in relation to the matrix of goods that establishes his sense of self.

By contrast, the capitalist does have a use for his capital. Since he identifies himself with his capital, he needs to own the enterprise that acts as an outlet for his self-expression. At the same time, however, the capitalist faces difficulties if he tries to impose his personality (especially his personal needs) on his enterprise. For this reason, capital may not provide a particularly adequate vehicle for self-expression.

The health and well-being of an enterprise has little to do with the personal needs of particular individuals. Capital has specific purposes—to make a profit and to grow—that have nothing to do with individual personalities, their private needs, and their unique modes of life. For this reason, capital is ill-suited to express personality, including that of the capitalist.

To be sure, different executives and different management teams will lead firms in different directions, and with differing degrees of success. But this is less a matter of expressing their personalities and more a matter of skill (and possibly luck). In this regard, management is more of a trade or profession, and less an art form. Success depends on foresight, knowledge, and skill, not on the ability and urge to self-expression.

A manager can express his personality in the choice of and exercise of his vocation. Presumably, managers have different personalities than artists or teachers. But this expression of personality through a vocation does not involve imposing personality on an enterprise. As capitalism develops, the capitalist gives way to the manager. The firm grows beyond the personality of its original founder-owner; its purposes lose any special connection with anyone's personality.

The prominence of the modern corporation confirms this tendency. The public issue of shares not only formally separates ownership from use, it also distinguishes between the private property of the owners of capital and the property of the capital. Limited liability means that the obligations incurred by the firm cannot affect the private property of shareholders. If a firm goes bankrupt, the shares of its owners lose their value, but their other property remains intact.

The idea of limited liability expresses the distinction between personal property and property in capital. By incorporating, the owner of the capital simultaneously makes himself rich (by selling shares) and protects his private life (as a consumer) from his professional life as an entrepreneur.

As the corporation loses its connection to the personality of its owner, it ceases to have a legitimate use in our first sense. It cannot express personality or be integrated into modes of consumption. Its owners cannot use it in everyday life as they might a chair or a car. Instead, it remains locked away in a safe-deposit box, providing its owner with a source of income. Thus, if we define legitimate use as integration into a mode of consumption, and if we require legitimate use for the recognition of property right, then capital has no legitimate use for individuals. If we make it illegal to own capital, or place all capital into the hands of the state, we will not, thereby, violate any individual rights.

Will this conclusion also follow if we interpret legitimate use as a use that does not infringe on the rights of others? As we have seen, the primary use individuals have for their capital is to make or keep themselves rich. This leads to the following question: Does becoming or remaining rich infringe on the rights of others?

In order to fix our ideas, let us begin by considering some of the ways in which individual consumption can infringe on others. The fact that consumption is a social act should encourage us to think about the kinds of social practices that are or are not consistent with respect for individual rights.

Various forms of pollution provide examples of ways in which the use of property can infringe on the rights of others. If I drive a car that pollutes the air and endangers the health of others, my consumption of the car infringes on their right to life. We can even, by extension, attribute part of the responsibility for this violation of rights to the firm that manufactured the car.

The automobile example sounds forceful, but it is not clear cut. Those whose health has been endangered could move away from polluted areas. If they have this option, then pollution need not infringe on their right to life. Moving away from polluted areas may cause hardship and expense, or otherwise affect the individual's mode of life. If so, whether pollution infringes on individual rights depends on whether the individual's right to life implies a right to support a mode of life. This would mean that the individual has a right to at least some of the things he needs.

Another example may clarify this point. Assume for the moment that you own a house on a hill, and that out of your front window you enjoy a magnificent view of the Rocky Mountains. The owner of the land between you and the mountains decides to build a high-rise office building that will block your view. Do you have the right to prevent him from building his office complex, bearing in mind that to do so will significantly affect the value of his property (in a sense, you will be taking away some of that value)? Does he have the right to put up a building that will adversely affect the value (both aesthetic and pecuniary) of your property?

Your neighbor's decision to put up an office building affects your mode of life. It deprives you of the pleasure of viewing the Rocky Mountains from your living room window. This experience may be important to you; it may be integral to your personal identity. Your sense of self may be sustained by that feeling of unity with nature you cultivate by having a mountain view. But your neighbor's use of his property is only illegitimate if you have a right to those things that support your mode of life.

One way to establish such a right would be to broaden our interpretation of the individual's right to life. Our interpretation will depend on what life this right refers to. If the right to life refers only to biological life, it may prevent my neighbor from shooting me, but it cannot prevent him from ruining the view from my living room window. But if the right to life refers to life in society, the matter becomes considerably more complex. If I depend on society and cannot live outside my social relations, especially my link with a socially defined sense of self, this second interpretation of my right to life takes on added force.

In this case, my right to life may require others to respect my mode of life. I have lived on a hill with a mountain view for many years. It has become an important part of my idea of who I am. I have established a right to continue to live this way. If deprived of my view, I will suffer a diminution of self. If I have this kind of right to continue an established mode of life that supports a well-developed personal identity, I may well have what two economists in a somewhat different context refer to as rights in the status quo.[11] I thus can legitimately prevent my neighbor from putting up his office building.

We have already suggested inconsistencies between private enterprise and the individual's right to those things that support his mode of life. But private enterprise is consistent with rights in the status quo so long as we interpret those rights in a preventive sense. In other words, I can prevent you from taking certain steps that will adversely affect my mode of life (such as obstructing my view of the mountains), but I cannot demand that I be provided with the things I need (such as a mountain view) simply because they could be part of my mode of life.

Because private enterprise encourages and requires change and development, it cannot recognize rights in the status quo indefinitely. The more we support preservation of older ways of life, the more we impede the development of new methods of production and modes of consumption. In the limit, we destroy the rationale for private enterprise. However, before we reach that limit, we can accept the right of individuals to slow down the process of change in order to preserve, at least for a period, an established mode of life.

The more we accept individual rights to preserve modes of life, the more we slow down the process of economic development. If we accept both the right to preserve a mode of life and the legitimacy of private enterprise, it becomes vitally important that we define the limits to this slowing down process. The importance of defining limits to rights in the status quo holds when we accept the necessity of change in modes of life, whether stimulated by private enterprise or not.

The fact that private enterprise does not support our right to the things we need does not establish whether private enterprise violates rights, or whether individuals have no right to the things they need. Private enterprise either takes precedence over, or stands in the way of, such rights. In order to find out which is the case, we need to find out if my becoming or remaining rich infringes the rights of others.

The obvious candidates for those infringed on are those who do not become rich. One argument, which originated with Marx, uses the idea that those who become rich by owning capital do so by "exploiting" those who do not own capital and who do not become rich. Marx's use of the term exploitation does not, however, bring into question the capitalist's property right over the profit that his capital yields. On the contrary, Marx seems to think that within the framework of a private enterprise economy, capitalists normally acquire their income through strict adherence to the prevailing principles of justice and ideas of individual rights.[12]

Private enterprise does not seem to require the violation of the property rights of others (through some form of exploitation). Only if we interpret the right to life as a right to maintain a particular mode of life will private enterprise come into conflict, at least in certain cases, with the right to life. The interpretation of the right to life as a right to maintain a mode of life may or may not be compelling. It could simply require that no one take my life away, rather than implying a social obligation to supply me with the things I need. If we leave aside the right to life, what other right could come into play in a consideration of private enterprise? To answer this question, we need to look more closely at the way in which the work of one individual to make himself rich can affect others.

We use capital to become rich, but (usually) not because we need to be rich in order to satisfy particular needs. Instead, our acquisition of capital helps us to enhance our social position. Our purpose is not simply to become rich, but to become rich relative to others.[13] In other words, we use capital to attain and enhance our position in a social hierarchy. We do this because of the importance our position in the social hierarchy has for our idea of who we are; it is an element of our personality structure.

Our position in the hierarchy of wealth provides us with a measure of our worth. The hierarchy establishes that individuals are of greater or lesser worth. Does recognition of an individual as a person of lower status (worth) violate his rights? This would be the case if an individual has a right to equal regard.[14] The demand that people be treated with equal regard limits property rights to capital in much the same way that the right to life limits property rights to objects such as weapons specifically designed to deprive people of their lives.

We need to emphasize that the right to equal regard only requires equality in a specific sense. It does not require that, for example, I be considered the equal of Luciano Pavarotti as an opera singer, or the equal of Albert Einstein as a physicist. It only requires that we all be considered equal as persons. But to be considered equal as persons means that we are treated in accord with the idea of persons. We can in effect drop the notion of equality without loss of meaning.[15] We retain the notion of equal regard because we live in a society in which some people are not treated altogether as persons. So, we must assert that they should be. The notion of equality carries weight when we attribute sameness to different things. In the following we retain the notion of equal regard, bearing in mind that it means nothing more than to regard as a person.

Of course, we do apply the idea of equal regard within our legal system, and (at least in principle) to political decisionmaking. The ideas of equality before the law and one man, one vote depend on our conviction that a just society treats all people the same within certain institutions. The idea of equal regard has not, however, been considered applicable to economic affairs, although many individuals have pointed out how economic inequality can undermine equality before the law and political equality.[16] Indeed, the dangers economic inequality pose to our political and legal rights can contribute to a powerful argument against private enterprise.

We can also make the argument directly, without reference to politics and law. If we have a right to equal regard, and if the use of capital as private property creates a hierarchy of differential regard, then the use of capital for private ends violates rights.

This conclusion depends heavily on the idea that we become rich not primarily in order to satisfy particular needs, but in order to be rich. Historically, the two purposes tend to become confused. Until recently, the freedom that a measure of wealth provides us to articulate and develop our personalities through modes of consumption was available only to a small group. As a result, to be rich was to be free. The rich were regarded as superior partly because they alone could afford the luxury of an individualized mode of consumption that emphasized their individual needs. Those who were free to express and develop their personalities through their modes of life also occupied a superior position in a social hierarchy.

This confusion of individual freedom with position in a social hierarchy had important implications. In particular, it restricted the way in which those who had wealth could develop and express their personalities. The requirements of establishing and maintaining their social position governed their modes of consumption in large part. Access to ritualized patterns of dress and behavior marked class differences in modes of life. Far from being really free to develop an individual mode of consumption, the true aristocrat worked hard to adhere to an established mode of life.

The socially defined hierarchy of wealth and status takes precedence over individual self-expression for those aspiring to occupy a position of superior regard. The objects they consume must establish their social position. Since individuality does not, in and of itself, involve social position, its demands can conflict with this objective. The confusion of wealth with freedom tended to hide the possibility of separating individual freedom from position in a social hierarchy. The individual freedom separated out in this way certainly requires a measure of wealth, but it does not require the pursuit of wealth for its own sake.

If our argument in the earlier part of this chapter concerning the ways of life associated with capital is correct, then the only use for capital that requires private ownership is self-aggrandizement. It follows that the real purpose served by private ownership of capital is pursuit of a position in a hierarchy of differential regard obtained by access to accumulations of wealth beyond need. In this case, private ownership over capital subverts our aspirations to live in a society based on the idea of equal regard. If we respect the right to equal regard, then neither criteria of legitimate use requires that we respect the individual's right to own capital. The absence of private ownership over capital does not mean the eclipse of private property and individual freedom.

The argument regarding the implications of private ownership of capital works against claims that private enterprise accords with the fundamental principles of justice, but it does not directly establish any form of state ownership as either just in itself or more just than private ownership. In order to establish a definite conclusion regarding private enterprise, it is also necessary to demonstrate that state ownership does not exacerbate the problems implied by private ownership of capital, or create other equal or more serious impediments to individual self-determination. Such a demonstration, while of critical importance to the issued treated here, takes us beyond the limits of this essay.

We have found two kinds of rights capable of providing a basis for restricting the use, and even ownership, of property: the right to support a mode of life and the right to equal regard. Thus far, we have given no reasons to support the existence of such rights, but we have indicated how they might affect our evaluation of the institutions of private enterprise.

As we have seen, we can broadly interpret the right to a mode of life. It may involve no more than the individual's right to preserve an established way of life against the encroachment of others (e.g., stopping my neighbor from obstructing my view of the mountains). Or, the right to a mode of life may place obligations on society to provide individuals with some, or all, of the things they need. Obviously, the broader our interpretation of the right to a mode of life, the more that right will come into conflict with the idea that income should depend on property ownership and with the institutions of private enterprise.

Recognition of a right to equal regard has very serious implications for private ownership of capital. Indeed, as we have interpreted this right, it cannot be consistent with the use of capital to achieve the private ends of its owners. In the epilogue, we will consider, in a preliminary manner, some of the reasoning that supports the ideas of a right to a mode of life and a right to equal regard.

EPILOGUE:
NEEDS
and RIGHTS

In recent years, the debate over public policy has increasingly adopted the language of rights: abortion rights, welfare rights, human rights, the rights of the handicapped, etc. The dependence of an individual or group on society no longer leads to an appeal to the goodwill of others or of society. The more firmly the idea of rights takes hold as a basis for the determination of policy, the more claims on the part of individuals and groups become demands that their rights be respected. In effect, individuals and groups now use the language of rights to translate their needs into social obligations. When they do so, they participate in a process that blurs the distinction between need and right. If a need creates a right, then how can we distinguish between the two?

On a semantic level, the distinction between need and right relates to the difference between a requirement of life and how that requirement gets fulfilled: need refers to the requirement, right to how we fulfill it. But if need creates a right, then whenever we find a need we also find a right. This means that we can use the terms need and right interchangeably.

Since rights have to do with how we satisfy needs, we cannot separate the concepts altogether. In order to understand the real distinction between the two, we need to follow a different route. Where no needs exist, the issue of rights does not arise. But simply because a need exists, we cannot conclude that an appeal to rights is relevant. Since rights are concerned with how we satisfy our needs, we may only have a right to satisfy certain needs; i.e., we can satisfy only certain needs at our will. If the term right refers to a special way of satisfying our needs, what kinds of needs do we have a right to satisfy?

When we exercise our rights, we engage in the work of exercising, expressing, or realizing our initiative. For example, it is important that the way in which we use our property be up to us because we use it to express who we are: our distinctive, individual qualities. By contrast, it is equally important that the way in which we maintain public health and safety not be a matter of private initiative. We do not exercise our sense of self by determining when, how, and if we personally would like to have our garbage collected or our streets cleaned.

The objects that satisfy our needs at our will (which we have a right to use to satisfy our needs) are our property. Economics tells us how we acquire the property that we need but do not already own—how we make things our property.

When we acquire the things we need through use of our property as means of exchange (when we sell our labor for our income), then our ability to satisfy our needs will depend on our property. Private enterprise makes need satisfaction contingent in this way. The only right that we have to satisfy our needs stems from property right—our right to use the property we own to satisfy our needs. If we allow private ownership of capital, then we can only acquire the things we need from others who own them. The reason for this is that private ownership of the means of production means that all newly produced goods will already be owned by those who owned the capital that produced them. In a private enterprise economy, distribution follows from property ownership. This makes property right the only right relevant to need satisfaction.

Only when we bring into question the legitimacy of the institutions of private enterprise can we begin to pose the question of how to distribute wealth. Without private ownership of capital, the distribution of newly produced wealth cannot be directly determined by the distribution of existing property (i.e., in the means of production). We require, in this case, a principle for determining the distribution of newly produced wealth. One such principle, although by no means the only one, resolves the problem by appealing to needs and allocating wealth according to need.

In Chapter 5, we found that the problem of private enterprise involves two questions: (1) Do we have a right to a mode of life? (2) Does our right to own property include the right to use our property to produce wealth (i.e., a right to own capital)? This second question implies another: Does the principle of equal regard apply to the distribution of wealth, and if so, does it take precedence over our right to use our property to make ourselves rich? When posed in this way, the problem of private enterprise adopts the form of a conflict over rights. Our decision concerning the legitimacy of private enterprise will depend on which rights prevail. How can we resolve conflict such as this between opposing rights?

In order to resolve this conflict, we need to say something more about where those rights that bear on our economic activities come from. Thus far, we have emphasized the link between such rights and needs associated with the individual's interest in defining a distinctive personal identity (his self-interest). We respect economic rights because we accept the necessity that the satisfaction of certain needs be left to us. By determining what we need and how we go about satisfying our needs, we determine ourselves.

This idea of self-determination makes the idea of freedom meaningful. Freedom does not mean the absence of determination; it means the self-determination of the individual within society and on the basis of social meaning and social practice. This social determination of the individual excludes his determination by any other individuals acting on the basis of their self-interest. The idea of rights enters at the point where we assert the importance of self-determination and exclude other individuals from determining our lives. Only when the satisfaction of certain kinds of needs is up to us can we be persons in the full sense of the term. We can only develop as persons when our rights are respected. The answer to the question where do our rights come from involves the development of an idea of what it takes to be a person and of the way in which individual self-determination takes place in society.[1]

Obviously, a full treatment of this issue would take us well beyond the limits we have imposed on the present discussion. We will, however, conclude our treatment of needs, rights, and the market by summarizing some of the more important conclusions that relate to the origin of rights, especially property rights.

1. Only to the extent that we think of the needs associated with developing and expressing a sense of self as true requirements of life can we make strong claims about our right to the things we need. Whims and desires do not lead us to rights; we can hardly claim a right to property based on whims.[2]

2. Assuming that we use property to satisfy real needs, it follows that we develop a special relation with our property. This is the relation of consumption. We consume goods by integrating them into a mode of consumption that realizes or expresses our mode of life. Our mode of life depends on our sense of self—the idea of personal identity that organizes and gives meaning to the way we lead our lives. By integrating property into our mode of life, we simul-

taneously establish the social meaning of our sense of self and give that property a special meaning within our overall consumption pattern. The integration of a good into our way of life establishes it as our property—something having a unique relationship with our personalities.

3. Since we need property to develop and express our personalities, we would like to claim a right to the things we need on the basis of that need. The first obstacle standing in the way of this claim is the overall amount of wealth available and the competing claims of others. The nature of this obstacle depends on how we view the origin, or production, of wealth. In our discussion of the factors of production, we considered two approaches to the problem of the production of wealth: (1) The amount of wealth is fixed by the available supply of resources (especially land and labor). We called this the standpoint of scarcity. The standpoint of scarcity seriously impedes the claim we would like to make that we have a right to the things we need. (2) The amount of wealth depends on the use of wealth as means of production (capital). Our ability to satisfy needs depends, in this second case, not on the availability of scarce resources, but on our devotion to using wealth to make wealth and our know-how concerning the production of wealth. We called this the standpoint of wealth. The standpoint of wealth makes it possible for us to claim a right to the things we need since it makes our ability to satisfy needs adaptable.[3]

4. The development of a private enterprise economy brings with it a vast expansion of wealth. One of the driving forces behind this process is the expansion and multiplication of needs. The development of modes of consumption creates space for the marketing of new products that underwrites profit making and the accumulation of capital. On the side of fixity of supply, private enterprise and the standpoint of scarcity have little in common.

5. The problem of private enterprise resolves itself into a clash between the right of the individual to define his personality on the basis of the goal of accumulating wealth (the right to own capital), and the right to equal regard: on one side, the right to use your property as the means to attain a position in a status hierarchy, on the other, the right to be treated as a person. The right to own capital implies the right to make significant demands on the self-regard of others—the right to include their relative social position within your own self-conception. Thus, when we interpret the right to own capital as a right to pursue and attain social status, respect for that right implicates others and intrudes on their work of self-determination.

If our attempt to attain position within a hierarchy of persons undermines equal regard, then it cannot adequately support individual self-determination. In applying the principle of equal regard, we need to emphasize that our interpretation of equal regard means treatment in accordance with the idea of a person. Thus, we treat each other equally because we treat each other in accordance with a commonly held idea of individual integrity and self-determination.

The more we preoccupy ourselves with the goal of achieving social status, the more our identity depends on the way others perceive us in relation to themselves. When we eliminate concern for relative social position, we open up the possibility that the individual can achieve self-determination to a degree not otherwise possible. To this extent, respect for the right to equal regard underwrites individual self-determination.

By distinguishing our modes of consumption and, therefore, our modes of life, we establish our individual identities on the basis of our unique set of needs. But while we may be different persons, we must each in our own way work to live according to the ideal associated with being a person. We respect the integrity of others, and command their respect for our integrity. Thus, our differences do not affect our expectation that others will treat us with due regard. Our ways of being individuals are just that, different modes of life, not different degrees of success in attaining the status of a person. In principle, then, no single scale exists that allows us to measure and rank our modes of life.

Private enterprise attempts to provide us with such a scale. It uses the value of the individual's property to translate individual differences in ways of life into differences in status within a measurable hierarchy. This translation leads to a contradiction that defines the problem of private enterprise. Private enterprise rests on the premise that we can be equal as persons while we strive to be unequally persons. The conflict between the two parts of this premise create stresses within capitalist society that regularly threaten to undermine the conditions for stable social reproduction.

Because private enterprise uses property to measure social position, modes of consumption take on a quantitative meaning: they signify amounts of wealth rather than qualities of individual personality. Acquisition and use of, for example, an expensive car establishes our relative social position insofar as the cost of the car excludes others from the associated mode of consumption. To the extent that consumption takes on this quantitative significance, it contributes only one thing to our sense of self: measurement of our position in a hierarchy.

Private enterprise uses the notion of quantitative hierarchy to reconcile the two poles of its basic premise. All the individuals within a quantitative hierarchy differ in degree and not in kind: they are all persons, but they are unequally so. But is a person the sort of thing we can be to different degrees? Can we preserve fully our status as persons and still be more or less so, superior and inferior? To the extent that we think that personal integrity requires respect of others, we cannot reconcile the integrity of our persons with the idea that we may be inferior persons. Personal integrity cannot survive without the due regard that hierarchies of wealth work to undermine. For this reason, the right to equal regard must take precedence. Without it, the integrity of the individual cannot be assured, and the entire system of rights will falter.

The integrity of the individual also suffers when we refuse him access to those things he needs to realize his personality. But defense of private enterprise assures that individuals will not have access to at least some of the things they need. The reason why private enterprise refuses to provide the individual with the things that he needs has to do with the way in which it encourages hierarchies of wealth and status. Such hierarchies presuppose that we preclude some individuals from access to certain modes of consumption, and encourage all individuals to aspire to attain those modes of consumption. Consider how quickly the satisfaction of being rich would dissipate if no one wanted to be rich, or cared that you were.

Respect for rights defends the integrity of the individual. The idea of equal regard expresses a commitment to that integrity. It defends the individual's right to self-determination. Individual freedom requires that we be free not from social determination, but from determination by other individuals. The principle of equal regard protects that freedom.

The principle of equal regard provides a basis for us to claim a right to acquire some of the things we need (those associated with our self-interest). A problem arises, however, when we assert this right within the cultural, political, legal, and historical framework of a private enterprise system. As we have seen, that framework encourages us to define ourselves in relation to the wealth and status of others. By so doing, it encourages needs identified with pursuit of relative social position. Such needs are not limited in a way that makes our claim to rights over property based on need sustainable. Thus, while private enterprise undermines the standpoint of scarcity on the side of the supply of wealth by encouraging the process of economic growth and development, it lends support to that standpoint on the side of demand by encouraging the limitless expansion of needs and the pursuit of wealth as an end in itself. So long as our needs are formed within this framework, we cannot have a right to the things that satisfy them.

This means that if we attempt to provide everyone with the things they need, we will soon run out of wealth, and we will do so before all needs can be satisfied. So long as needs remain influenced by hierarchies of status, our right to the things we need will remain a utopian aspiration.

This does not mean that the principle of equal regard must fall by the wayside. Society can assert principles and protect rights, some of whose social and individual preconditions remain unfulfilled. We can define intermediate goals. One such intermediate goal translates equal regard into a right to income. Standing behind the idea of a right to income is the idea that everyone should have fair access to the limited supply of wealth, and that each individual, given his income, should determine the specific means of consumption (those components of social wealth) most appropriate to his private ends.

If we take the idea of a right to income one step further by distributing wealth equally among people, we get an additional result. In a society that measures status by income, equality of income implies equality of status (in effect, equal regard). This allows us to respect individual self-determination and the principle of equal regard in a society that cannot fully satisfy the needs of individuals. Assertion of the principle of equal distribution tends to weaken the forces stimulating the expansion of needs insofar as those stem from hierarchies of wealth and to lead us to a point where the rationing of wealth through income becomes unnecessary. At that point, the integrity of the individual and his self-determination fully displace pursuit of position in a social hierarchy; the problem of private enterprise disappears.

Obviously, we remain some distance from this goal. But in the struggle over public policy, we can already clearly discern the outlines of the problem—the conflict over rights—and the terms of the solution. In order to assure that we achieve a solution to social problems consistent with individual self-determination, we must clarify the meaning of, and necessary conditions for, individual integrity. This requires that we call into question the simplistic identification of freedom with the free market and of property rights with the right to own capital.

NOTES

1. The idea that pursuit of the public good requires appeal to reasoned argument underlies John Rawls's notion of a "reflective equilibrium" resulting from the "exercise of thought" under "conditions favorable for deliberation" (1971, p.48). Ronald Dworkin interprets this idea to imply "a theory of a community," which provides the basis for a "group consideration of problems of justice" (1977, p.163).

2. See Arrow (1951) for a classic example of this approach.

3. See Levine (1977, Chap. 1).

4. For a more detailed discussion of this point, see Levine (1981, Chap. 7, esp. pp. 299–300).

5. Recent contributions to political and moral theory seek to take into account the idea of personality: see Williams (1976) and Feinberg (1980). In order to incorporate determinate needs, we must move beyond the formalism of moral theory as embodied in such notions as the "capacity for moral personality" (Rawls, 1980). When we root needs in personality structure and the idea of the self, we exclude the idea that persons "choose" their life plans with "deliberative rationality" as suggested by Rawls (1971, p. 421).

6. I am indebted to Lynn Levine for pointing out the link between personality structure and biography.

7. Our treatment of the relation of need to the idea of the self owes much to the work of Heinz Kohut (1977). Kohut relates the sense the person has of being a "center of initiative and perception," thus an autonomous or self-determining being, to the cohesiveness

of an "enduring psychic configuration" (pp. 177–178). Kohut's work emphasizes the integrity (cohesiveness) of the self, and especially the implications of a loss of integrity (pp. 117, 128–139). Feinberg (1980, p.9) notes that autonomy fails if it lacks "internal order and structure." For our autonomy to be real, it must exist as the animating principle of a mode of life and give meaning and coherence to a structure of needs. This means that autonomy, freedom, and self-determination lose their meaning unless they constitute a cohesive and enduring personality. We use the term integrity to capture this connection.

8. Taylor (1976) refers to a "conflict of self-interpretations" in the context of the analysis of decisionmaking. For use of the term choice that is consistent with the conception of the person and his needs put forward here, see Kohut (1977, p.283).

9. As we emphasized earlier, our needs and the structure of the self that defines them do not appear immediately fully developed but emerge out of a process of self-seeking and self-development. Because of this, my idea of myself can incorporate inconsistencies and contradictions; it can be more or less well integrated, more or less capable of being consistently lived within society. Thus, it may not be possible to express my sense of self as a simple idea or set of ideas. For this reason, when we use the term idea of the self, we have in mind a whole self-conception implicit and explicit. It follows that our notion of a socially defined sense of self differs from the sociological notion that people adopt "roles" in society.

10. See Kohut (1977, p.81).

11. For further discussion of this point, see Levine (1981, Chap. 7).

12. We use the term justice to mean the recognition of rights. Dworkin (1977, Chap. 6) argues for such a link between justice and rights when he attempts to show how Rawls's concept of justice depends on a "deeper theory" whose central idea is that of right. Obviously, the identification of right with justice raises serious questions. We cannot attempt to address these questions directly here. Our identification of justice with rights also identifies the idea of a well-ordered society with respect for the integrity of persons. When we associate a well-ordered society with respect for the integrity of persons, we also advance the claim that protection of rights assures fairness and the treatment of all persons with proper regard to what is due them as persons. The reader may be more comfortable with this claim if he bears in mind that we will interpret rights more broadly than usual and more broadly than argued, for example, by advocates such as Robert Nozick of a pure private

enterprise system.

13. In the following, we use the term "distribution" exclusively to connote a specific pattern of ownership claims over wealth.

14. Robert Nozick (1974, pp.149–150) emphasizes this point. His argument closely follows the logic of a pure private enterprise system.

15. See Rawls (1971 and 1980) and Scanlon (1982).

16. See Williams (1976, pp.200–201), and Feinberg (1980, p.20).

17. On the notions of natural rights and equal treatment, see Dworkin (1977, pp.176–182).

18. Rawls argues that the " principles of justice define a partial ideal of the person" (1971, p.261). The more clearly we identify respect for persons with respect for their rights (Feinberg 1981, p.151), the more closely we identify the issue of rights with the determination of the requirements of personhood. One way to distinguish theories of right is according to the concreteness or determinacy of their underlying concept of persons. Nozick's theory lies at one extreme, because it provides the thinnest theory of the person. Rawls goes further while retaining the idea that "within wide limits" the theory of justice "does not prejudge the choice of the sort of persons that men want to be" (1971, p.260). Our own approach respects the requirements of self-determination and sustains the differences among persons while adding considerably to the content of the notion of the person. Naturally, this must lead to further restriction on the sorts of persons that men might want to be (see Chap. 5).

19. For a critique of the positivist arguments that make right dependent on law, see Dworkin (1977) and Lyons (1984, p.129).

20. On this aspect of the right to freedom of expression, see Scanlon (1975, p.186).

21. In the *Philosophy of Right,* Hegel goes further than Kant (and the Kantian tradition) in specifying the concept of a person and therefore the concept of an ethical order (of persons) as implied by the idea of right; see Ritter (1982).

CHAPTER 2

1. If the meaning of a word is found in the way we use it, then an object is nothing more or less than the social practice within which it is defined; see Wittgenstein (1953).

2. The distinction between need and right realizes concretely the idea that justice entails treating persons in accord with the idea of a person and thus with due regard for them as ends rather than

means. For this reason, the distinction does not have meaning within the utilitarian theory.

3. We leave aside for the moment issues that arise where my consumption directly impinges on the rights of others. We return to these issues in Chapter 5.

4. Locke (1955, Chap. 5).

5. Ibid.

6. See Smith (1937, Book I).

7. Sahlins (1972, Chap. 1).

8. See Hobbes (1958, Chap. 10). Authority refers to attributes of positions and only of persons in their capacity as occupants of positions.

CHAPTER 3

1. Francois Quesnay in Meek (1963, p.207).

CHAPTER 4

1. See Levine (1980) for a fuller discussion of classical price theory.

2. This point is noted by Koopmans (1957, p.137). We consider it at greater length in Levine (1977, Chap. 6).

3. The argument in this section is intended to exemplify one important aspect of price determination. An obvious gap in the present discussion is the absence of consideration of the competition of capitals. For a more comprehensive and systematic treatment, see Levine (1981).

4. Veblen's discussion of "pecuniary emulation" (1899, Chap. 2) focuses on one of the central themes of our analysis of the market. We can see here how this concept bears on price determination and economic growth.

5. Scherer (1970, pp.72–103) summarizes discussion in economics of the relation of cost to scale.

6. See Cowling (1982, p.29).

7. Veblen (1899, pp.82–83).

8. Penrose (1959, pp.26–30) develops this idea as the basis for a conception of the growth of the firm.

CHAPTER 5

1. Robert Nozick identifies this condition with the idea of a "free society" (1974, pp.149–150). His argument does not take into account the distinction between means of production and means of consumption, and assumes that freedom requires private ownership of both.

2. Kant describes the state of nature as one "devoid of justice" and argues against the idea that by entering society men sacrifice part of their freedom (1970, pp.137, 140). For a discussion of the difference between Kant and Locke on this point, see Murphy (1970, pp.113–127).

3. We make this assumption in order to sustain the argument regarding distribution. Its weakness is a weakness at the core of that argument. In our own treatment of the market, we assumed that firms follow a different logic.

4. This idea of the capitalist provides a foundation for Marx's notion of class. Max Weber (1958) presents an especially vivid historical account.

5. "[S]urvival and social dominance can be at the price of the abandonment of the core of the self and lead, despite seeming victory, to a sense of meaninglessness and despair" (Kohut 1977, p.117).

6. "In the nature of the case, the desire for wealth can scarcely be satiated in any individual instance, and evidently a satiation of the average or general desire for wealth is out of the question. . . . [S]ince the struggle is substantially a race for reputability on the basis of an invidious comparison, no approach to a definitive attainment is possible" (Veblen 1899, p.39).

7. Criticism of Robert Nozick's argument focuses on one or another aspect of this issue. G. A. Cohen (1978) points out the way in which allowing the market to determine distribution leads to in-equalities of power with significant implications beyond the econ-omy. Thomas Scanlon (1981) emphasizes bounds on appropriation and argues that Nozick's claims regarding distribution are weakened when holdings extend beyond the conveniences of life.

8. John Finnis (1980, p.172) makes an argument regarding legitimate ownership of capital that is reminiscent of Keynesian theory when he asserts that "[t]he private owner of a natural re-source or capital good has a duty in justice to put it to productive use...." Finnis arrives at this conclusion by defining justice in a way that is radically different from Nozick. The Keynesian critique of pure private enterprise centers on its failure to utilize fully its own producing potential. By failing to do so, it stands in the way of the

common good. Finnis sees in this failure to support the common good a failure of justice.

9. This idea provides a starting point for otherwise radically diverse theories, including those of Nozick (1974), Rawls (1971, p.261), and Finnis (1980, p.223). This similarity clearly indicates the importance of a concrete theory of rights. Differences arise as soon as the theory addresses questions regarding the nature, origin, and limits of rights.

10. The distinction between Kant and Hegel involves the idea that ethical life constitutes the "institutional reality of human self-hood" (Ritter 1982, p.172). The relation of Kant to Hegel is further clarified in Richard Winfield's introduction to the collection of essays by Ritter.

11. Owen and Braeutigman (1978).

12. Furthermore, difficulties arise when we investigate Marx's idea that labor produces profit and is therefore exploited when the capitalists appropriate it as their income. This requires that we demonstrate that capital makes no contribution to the net product. We have criticized this idea elsewhere; see Levine (1978, pp.90–96, 198–212, 306–312).

13. The contractarian theory (especially Rousseau's) considers property in general the origin of inequality and therefore cannot separate unequal regard from civilized society. Marx sometimes reproduces this idea as a critique of property, although he also pursues the idea that capital generates and sustains inequality.

14. Dworkin argues that the right to "equal concern and respect" is the "fundamental concept" of the "deep theory" of Rawls's theory of justice (1977, p.181). In effect, this amounts to a claim that such a right constitutes the basis of an ethical order.

15. Bernard Williams (1962) points out the dangers and confusions we encounter when we use the notion of equality in contexts such as this.

16. See Lindblom (1977).

EPILOGUE

1. This is the point at which the Kantian roots of contemporary moral theory are most telling. A theory of right becomes a theory of social organization when we demand that it specify concretely the concept of a person and the ethical order required to sustain people. Dworkin emphasizes the link between rights and the condition of being treated as a person, but tells us very little about

the determinants of personhood. Rawls attempts to deduce the basic qualities of the institutions of a just society from the agreement of individuals endowed with the capacity for moral personality. Yet as Thomas Nagel (1975) points out, Rawls requires that agreement regarding basic institutions be arrived at by individuals unaware of their own conceptions of the good. This raises questions concerning whether Rawls's approach allows for a specification of persons adequate to moral argument; see also Rawls's 1980 essay (p.527).

2. This element is missing in Judith Thomson's otherwise pointed critique of Nozick. Thomson argues that needs can sometimes override rights and criticizes the notion of the "infinite stringency of rights" implicit in Nozick's arguments (Thomson 1981, pp. 136–137). To make her argument compelling we would have to specify more carefully the relation of need to right and the relation of one right to another. This calls for a theory of need and a concept of personality capable of grounding the specification of rights; otherwise, our criticism must appeal to degree of intensity of competing claims that can easily become subjective.

3. We have seen that the standpoint of wealth does not prevent us from considering the way in which the supply of wealth limits need satisfaction. This limit does, however, look different from the standpoint of wealth than it does from that of scarcity.

BIBLIOGRAPHY

Arrow, Kenneth. *Social Choice and Individual Values*. Yale University Press, 1951.

Cohen, G. A. "Robert Nozick and Wilt Chamberlain: How Patterns Preserve Liberty." In *Justice and Economic Distribution*. Ed. by John Arthur and William Shaw. Prentice-Hall, 1978.

Collingwood, R. G. *An Essay on Philosophical Method*. Oxford University Press, 1933.

Cowling, Keith. *Monopoly Capitalism*. Macmillan, 1982.

Douglas, Mary, and Baron Isherwood. *The World of Goods*. Norton, 1979.

Dworkin, Ronald. *Taking Rights Seriously*. Harvard University Press, 1974.

Feinberg, Joel. *Rights, Justice, and the Bounds of Liberty*. Princeton University Press, 1980.

Finnis, John. *Natural Law and Natural Rights*. Oxford University Press, 1980.

Hegel, G.W.F. *Hegel's Philosophy of Right* tr. by T. M. Knox. Oxford University Press, 1952.

Hobbes, Thomas. *Leviathan*. Bobbs-Merrill Company, 1958.

Kalecki, Michal. *The Theory of Economic Dynamics*. Monthly Review Press, 1978.

Kant, Immanuel. *Kant's Political Writings* ed. by Hans Reiss. Cambridge University Press, 1970.

Kohut, Heinz. *The Restoration of the Self*. International Universities Press, 1977.

Koopmans, T. C. *Three Essays on the State of Economic Science*. McGraw-Hill, 1957.

Levine, David. *Economic Studies.* Routledge & Kegan Paul, 1977.

———. *Economic Theory.* 2 vols. Routledge & Kegan Paul, 1978 and 1981.

———. "Aspects of the Classical Theory of Markets." *Australian Economic Papers* (June 1980):1–15.

Lindblom, Charles E. *Politics and Markets.* Basic Books, 1977.

Lyons, David. *Ethics and the Rule of Law.* Cambridge University Press, 1984.

Marx, Karl. *Capital.* 3 vols. International Publishers, 1967.

Meek, Ronald. *The Economics of Physiocracy.* Harvard University Press, 1963.

Murphy, Jefferie G. *Kant: The Philosophy of Right.* Macmillan, 1970.

Nagel, Thomas. "Rawls on Justice." In *Reading Rawls.* Ed. by Norman Daniels. Basic Books, 1975.

Nozick, Robert. *Anarchy, State and Utopia.* Harvard University Press, 1974.

Owen, B., and R. Braeutigman. *The Regulation Game.* Ballinger, 1978.

Penrose, Edith. *The Theory of the Growth of the Firm.* Basil Blackwell, 1959.

Rawls, John. *A Theory of Justice.* Harvard University Press, 1971.

———. "Kantian Constructivism in Moral Theory." *The Journal of Philosophy* 67:9 (September 1980).

Ricardo, David. *Principles of Political Economy and Taxation.* In P. Sraffa, ed. *Works and Correspondence of David Ricardo.* Vol. 1. Cambridge University Press, 1951.

Ritter, Joachim. *Hegel and the French Revolution.* Tr. by Richard Winfield. M.I.T. Press, 1982.

Robinson, Joan. *Essays in the Theory of Economic Growth.* St. Martin's Press, 1962.

Rousseau, J. J. "Discourse on the Origin and Foundations of Inequality." In *The First and Second Discourses.* Ed. by Roger Masters. St. Martin's Press, 1964.

Sahlins, Marshall. *Stone Age Economics.* Aldine, 1972.

Scanlon, Thomas. "Contractualism and Utilitarianism." In *Utilitarianism and Beyond.* Ed. by Amartya Sen and Bernard Williams. Cambridge University Press, 1982.

———. "Nozick on Rights, Liberty and Property." In Jeffrey Paul, ed. *Reading Nozick.* Rowman and Littlefield, 1981.

———. "Rawls Theory of Justice." In *Reading Rawls.* Ed. by Norman Daniels. Basic Books, 1975.

Scherer, F. M. *Industrial Market Structure and Economic Performance.* Rand McNally, 1970.

Schumpeter, J.A. *The Theory of Economic Development.* Harvard University Press, 1934.

Smith, Adam. *The Wealth of Nations.* Modern Library, 1937.

Sraffa, Piero. *The Production of Commodities by Means of Commodities.* Cambridge University Press, 1960.

Steindl, Josef. *Maturity and Stagnation in American Capitalism.* Basil Blackwell, 1952.

Taylor, Charles. "Responsibility for Self." In *The Identities of Persons.* Ed. by Amelie Rorty. University of California Press, 1976.

Thomson, Judith Jarvis. "Some Ruminations on Rights." In *Reading Nozick.* Ed. by Jeffrey Paul. Rowman and Littlefield, 1981.

Veblen, Thorstein. *The Theory of the Leisure Class.* Macmillan, 1899.

Weber, Max. *The Protestant Ethic and the Spirit of Capitalism.* Scribners, 1958.

Williams, Bernard. "Persons, Character and Morality." In *The Identities of Persons.* Ed. by Amelie Rorty. University of California Press, 1976.

————. "The Idea of Equality." In *Philosophy, Politics and Society.* 2d series. Ed. by Peter Laslett and W. G. Runciman. Oxford University Press, 1962.

Wittgenstein, Ludwig. *Philosophical Investigations.* Blackwell, 1953.

INDEX

ABOUT THE BOOK
and
THE AUTHOR

In *Needs, Rights, and the Market,* David Levine addresses primary concerns of economics from a novel starting point regarding the motivations of individuals. Levine develops a framework for exploring a set of questions central to political economy: What sorts of wants and needs are appropriate for us to satisfy through the use of markets? What is the nature of wealth? What rights do we have that bear on our economic activities? How do markets work and what is their social purpose? How can we justify private enterprise as a way of organizing need satisfaction, and what argument can we make against this type of social-economic organization? What is the relation between inequality of income and inequality of persons? His argument develops on the basis of an interpretation of individual wants influenced by contemporary psychoanalytic theory. The consequent treatment of consumption decisions provides the basis for important conclusions regarding price determination, capital accumulation, and income distribution.

Levine concludes by applying his analysis to the concepts of rights to income and to different types of property (including property in the means of production) and, generally, to the relationship of needs to rights. His nontechnical method, though involving a high level of abstraction, is accessible to readers with little background in economics.

David Levine is professor of economics in the Graduate School of International Studies, University of Denver. Previously, he was professor and chair of the university's Department of Economics and, prior to joining the DU faculty, was associate professor of economics at Yale University.